VELOCITY™

# How to Draw the Most Exciting, Awesome Manga

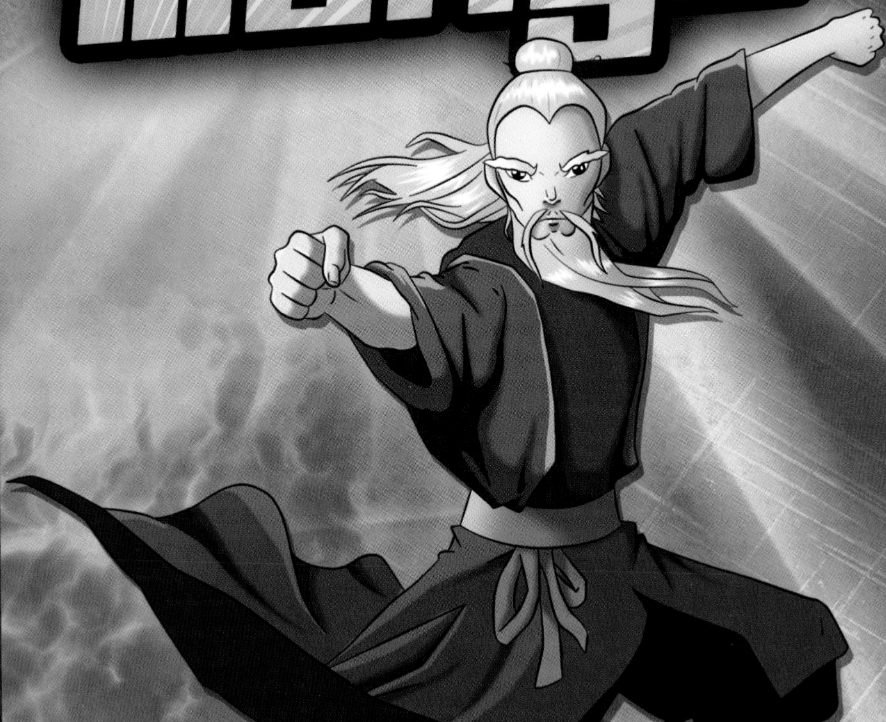

CAPSTONE PRESS
a capstone imprint

Velocity is published by Capstone Press,
151 Good Counsel Drive, P.O. Box 669, Mankato, Minnesota 56002.
www.capstonepress.com

Books published by Capstone Press are manufactured with paper
containing at least 10 percent post-consumer waste.

*Library of Congress Cataloging-in-Publication Data*
Singh, Asavari.
  How to draw the most exciting, awesome manga / by Asavari Singh.
  p. cm. — (Velocity : drawing)
  Includes bibliographical references.
  ISBN 978-1-4296-6593-3 (library binding)  1.  Comic books, strips, etc. — Japan—
Technique — Juvenile literature. 2.
  Cartooning—Technique—Juvenile literature.  I. Title. II. Series.

NC1764.5.J3S56 2012
741.5'1— dc22                                                    2011010505

**Editorial Credits**
**Author:** Asavari Singh
**Art Director:** Joita Das
**Designer:** Deepika Verma, Isha Khanna, Navneet Kaur
**Coloring Artists:** Aadil Ahmed Siddiqui, Abhijeet Sharma, Danish Zaidi,
                Priyanka Singh, Madhavi Poddar, Vinay Kumar Sharma
**Line Artists:** Deepak Kumar, Ishan Varma, Martin James, Nishant Mudgal,
                Prithwiraj Samat, Surendra Kumar Tripathi

Printed in the United States of America in Melrose Park, Illinois.
032011        006112LKF11

# TABLE OF CONTENTS

Chapter 1

# What is MANGA?

**Unique style, powerful poses, and amazing action are what manga comics are all about. They are packed with cool characters too, ranging from awesome warriors to fearsome robots and a whole lot more.**

Manga is a style of drawing that became popular in Japan in the 1940s. The word manga means “whimsical pictures” in Japanese, but this art form is about more than just drawing. It is also about storytelling, distinctive themes, and powerful characters. Today, manga is a worldwide phenomenon that you can be a part of too!

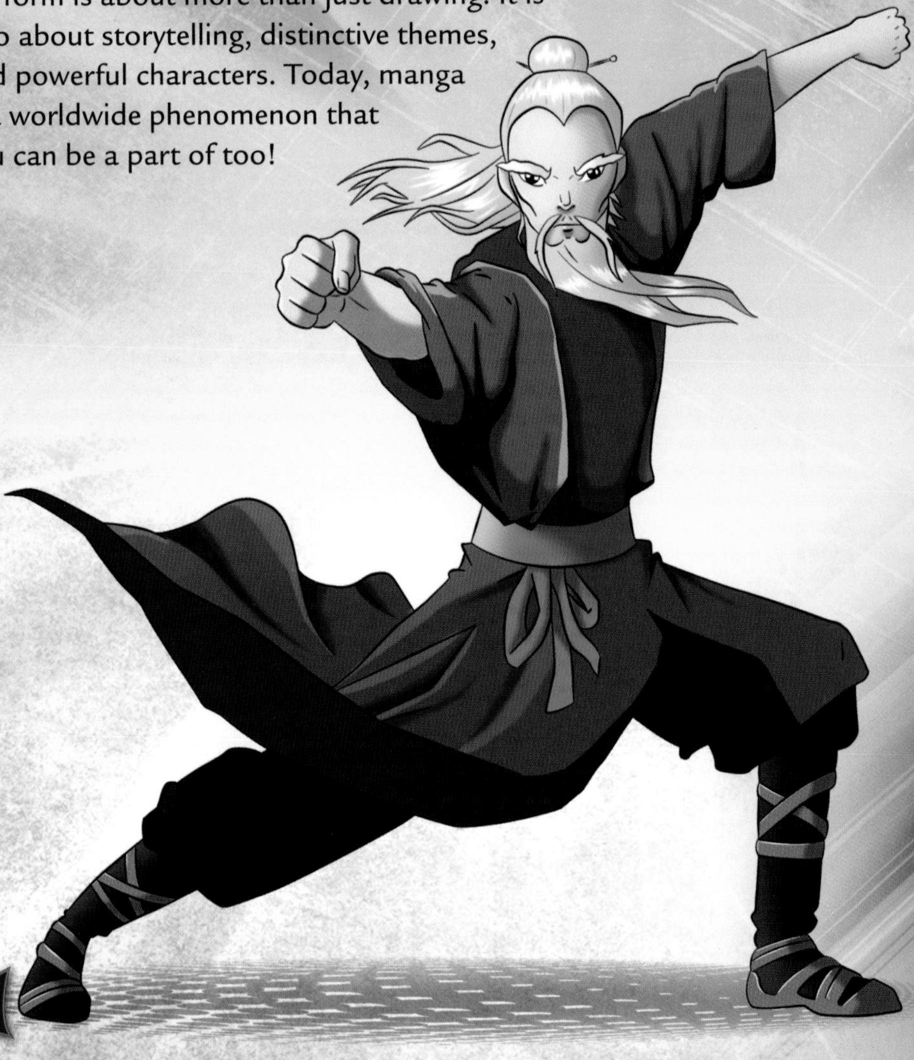

# All About Style

Manga characters have a very distinctive look. They are less realistic than other comic book characters. They usually have large eyes, small mouths, pointed chins, and funky, colorful hair.

**Fact**

The big, shiny eyes of manga characters were introduced by Japanese artists who were inspired by early Disney films like *Bambi*.

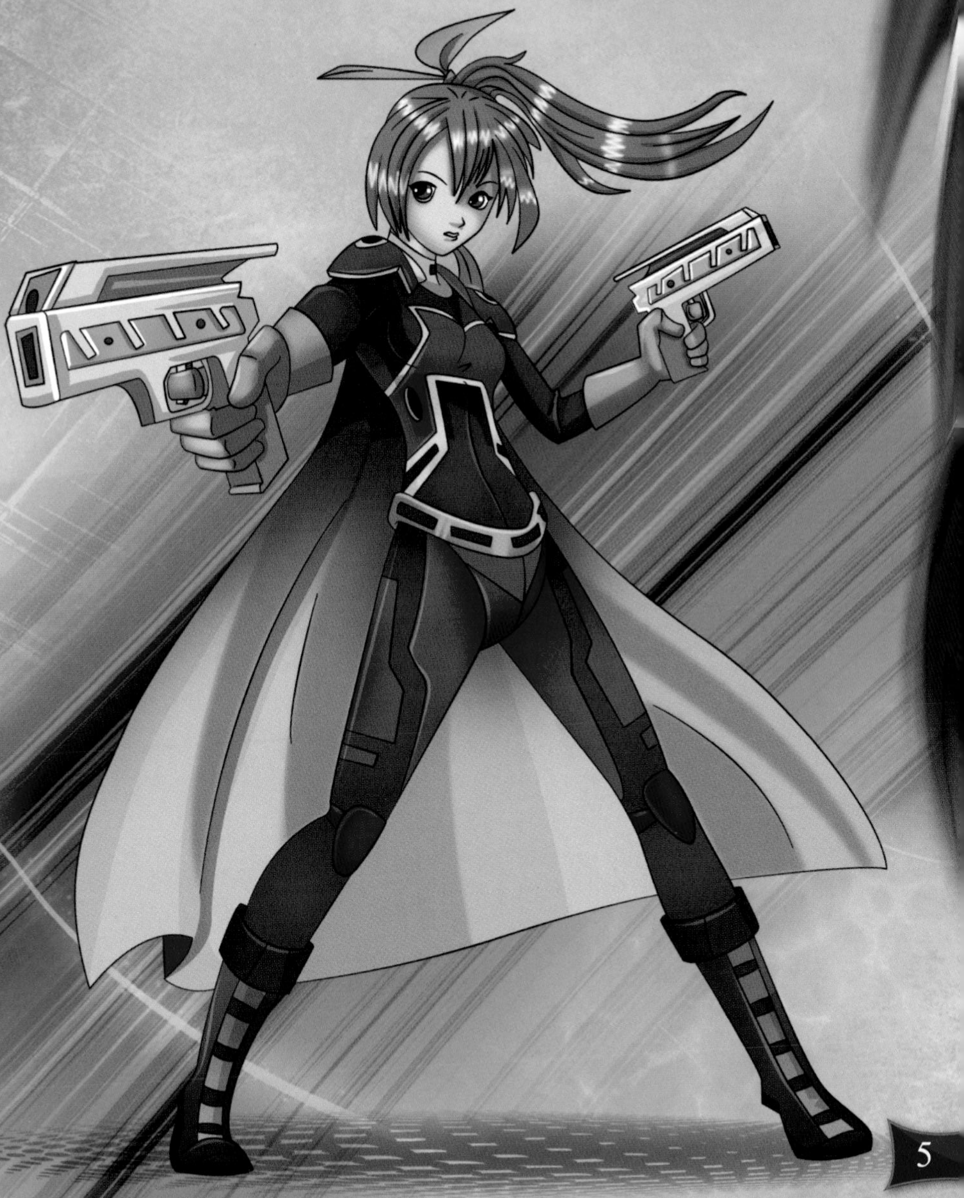

 **Chapter 2**

# Pieces and Parts

Let's start with the typical manga head. First you'll learn to draw the front and side views and see how features are placed. Then have fun with hairstyles and accessories!

## FRONT VIEW

1. Draw a circle and cut it in half with a vertical line. Then draw three lines to divide the head. Extend the vertical line to mark the chin's tip. Draw the jaw and neck.

2. Use the horizontal lines as guidelines for placing the hairline, eyebrows, eyes, and mouth.

3. Add details to the eyes. The nose and mouth come next —remember, these are never very detailed. Complete the outline of the hair.

4. Erase all unnecessary lines. Add more detail to the eyes and hair. You can even add highlights to the hair in typical manga style!

# PROFILE

**1** Draw a divided circle for the profile. This time, though, the chin will slant sideways from the circle. Add features and hair.

**2** Finish the eye and hair. Erase guidelines.

# HAIR

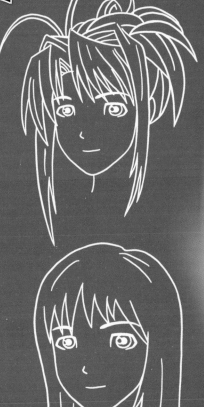

Hairstyles can tell you a lot about a manga character. Traditional down-to-earth characters usually have long straight hair. Young energetic characters often sport short, spiky hairstyles. The wilder the hair, the wilder the character's personality!

# Eyes and Expressions

The eyes are the most important part of a manga character's face. They really have to pop, so pay attention to detail. The nose and mouth are a breeze in comparison!

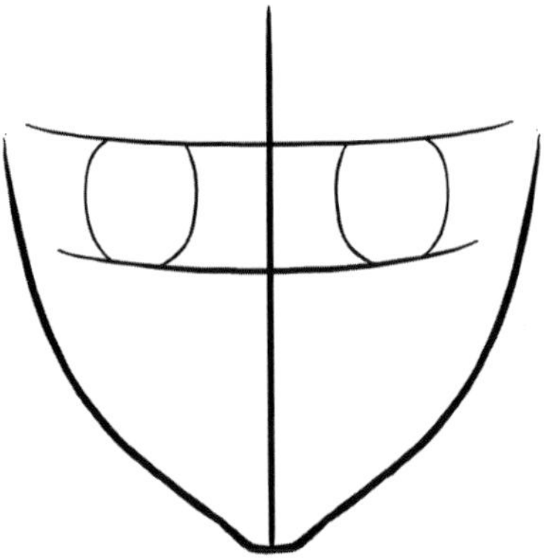

**1** Draw guidelines across the face. Then place two U shapes for the eyes on either side of the face.

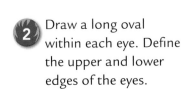

**2** Draw a long oval within each eye. Define the upper and lower edges of the eyes.

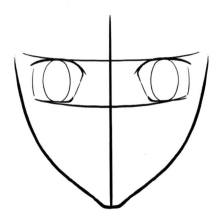

**3** Draw the eyebrows and define the upper lid as shown. Draw an oval within each oval. Add sparkle to the eyes by defining light glares in each eye.

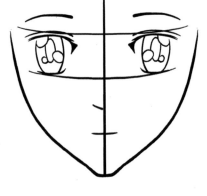

**4** Darken the eyes. Leave some parts white to show shine. Add sweeping eyelashes. Erase guidelines.

Show different emotions by adjusting the shape of the eyes and eyebrows.

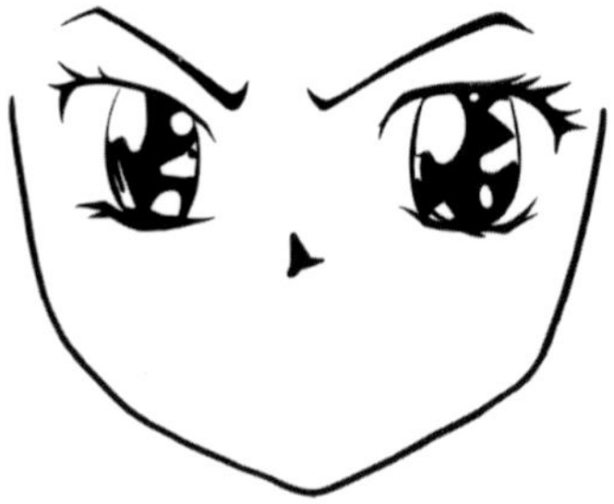

ANGRY

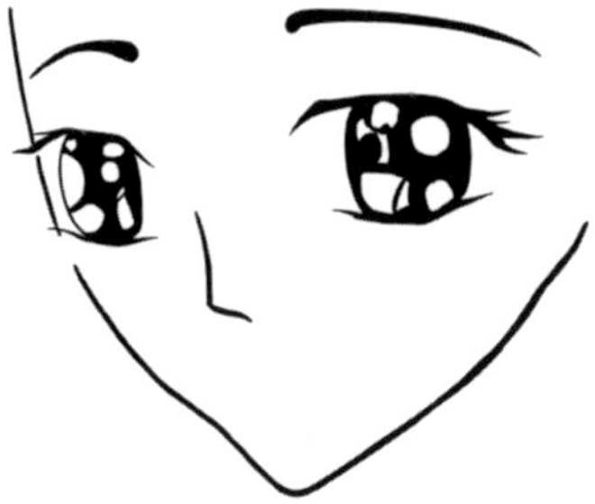

CALM

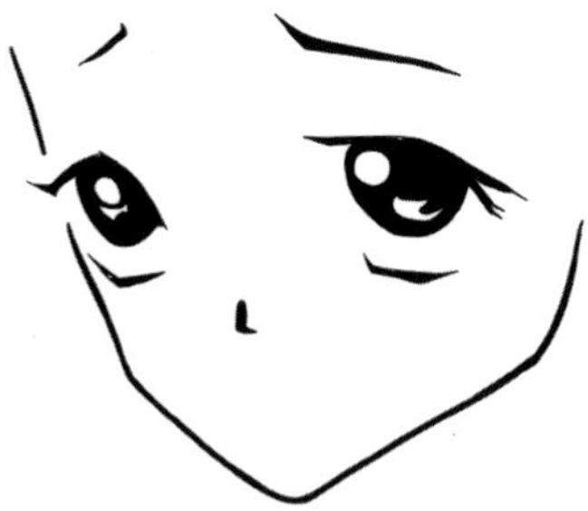

WORRIED

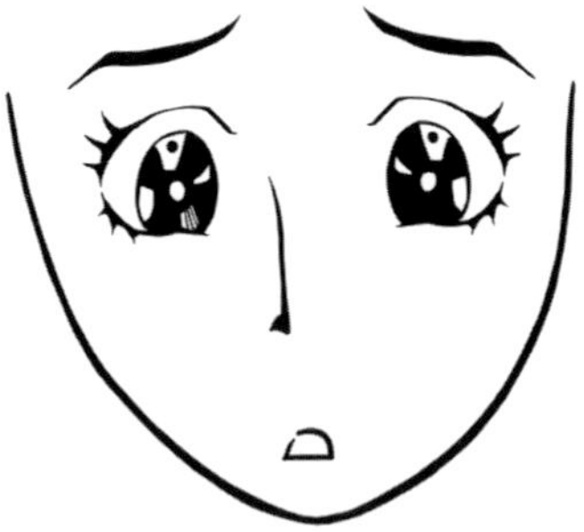

SHOCKED

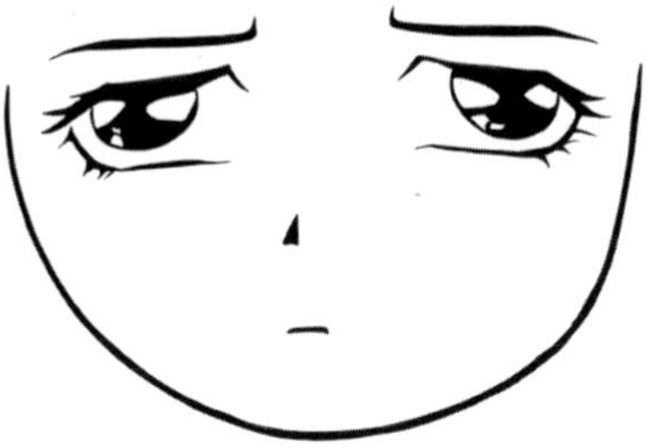

SAD

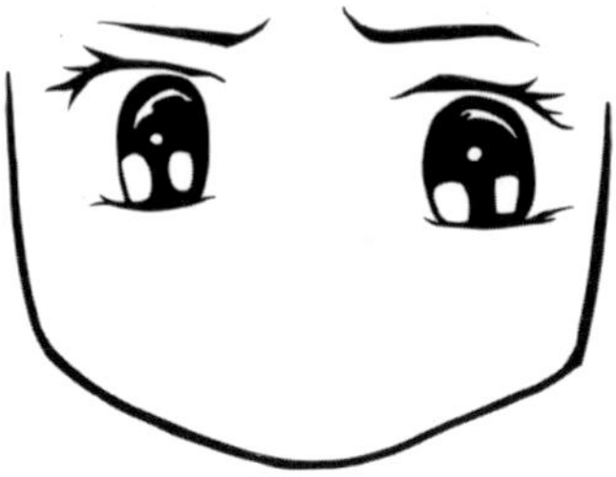

IRRITATED

## Tip

Males generally have narrower eyes than females, while children have the roundest peepers.

# Hands and Feet

Hands and feet can be a little tricky to draw. So practice making the basic shapes well. Once you do this, you'll be able to draw hands in many gestures and positions.

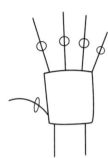

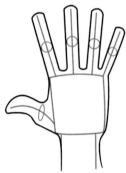

**1** Make a wireframe for the hand, with a square palm and circles for knuckles.

**2** Draw around the lines to flesh out the wireframe.

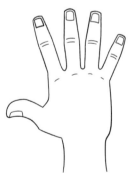

**3** Add details such as fingernails and knuckles.

Try these expressive gestures. Make sure you start with a wireframe.

Try to draw the foot from different angles. You can also dress it up with different kinds of footwear.

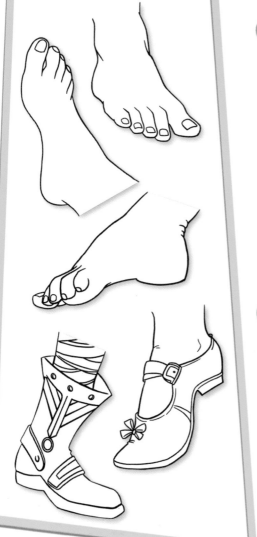

**1** Make a trapezium shape for the foot. It should be broadest at the toes. Draw a line for the ankle.

**2** Draw tube shapes around the lines for the toes. Draw arcs near the tips of the toes.

**3** Define the final shape of the leg and add details such as the toenails and heel.

trapezium: a four-sided shape that has only one pair of parallel lines

# Chapter 3

# Body Basics

A simple stick figure or wireframe is the skeleton of any manga body. It helps define the size, proportions, and shape of a character. You can then layer on all the flesh and fashion you want.

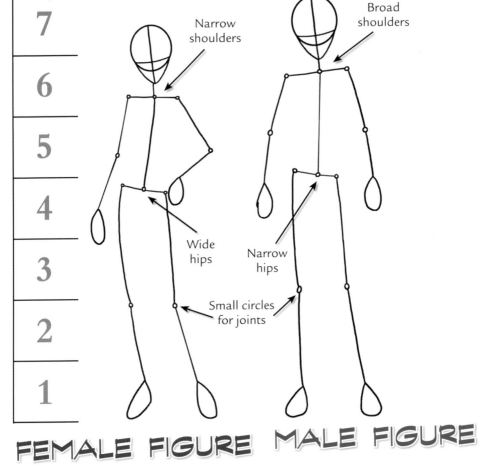

Narrow shoulders

Broad shoulders

Wide hips

Narrow hips

Small circles for joints

7

6

5

4

3

2

1

FEMALE FIGURE    MALE FIGURE

It's important to get your proportions right. Manga men are about seven heads tall, while women are around 6.5 heads tall.

**proportion:** the size of one part in relation to another

Flesh out your stick figures with solid shapes like spheres, cylinders, and curved rectangles. This will give them a three-dimensional look.

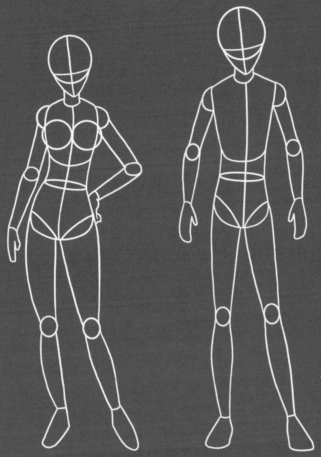

## Tips

- Don't use perfectly straight lines for human shapes. Lines will be more curved for female shapes.

- Use the joints to guide your proportions. The arms and legs will taper off from these points on the body.

- Read up on human anatomy and see pictures of how different muscles drape over the bones. This will help you draw more accurately.

sphere: a three-dimensional or solid circle, like a basketball

# Dynamic Posing

Experiment with the wireframe to create exciting action poses. This is known as dynamic posing.

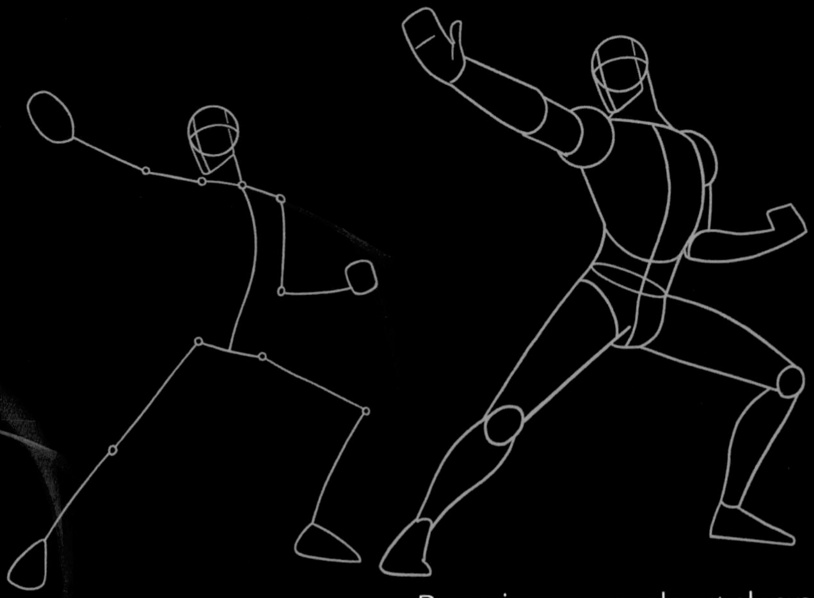

Dynamic poses are almost always drawn at an angle. This gives the character a three-dimensional look.

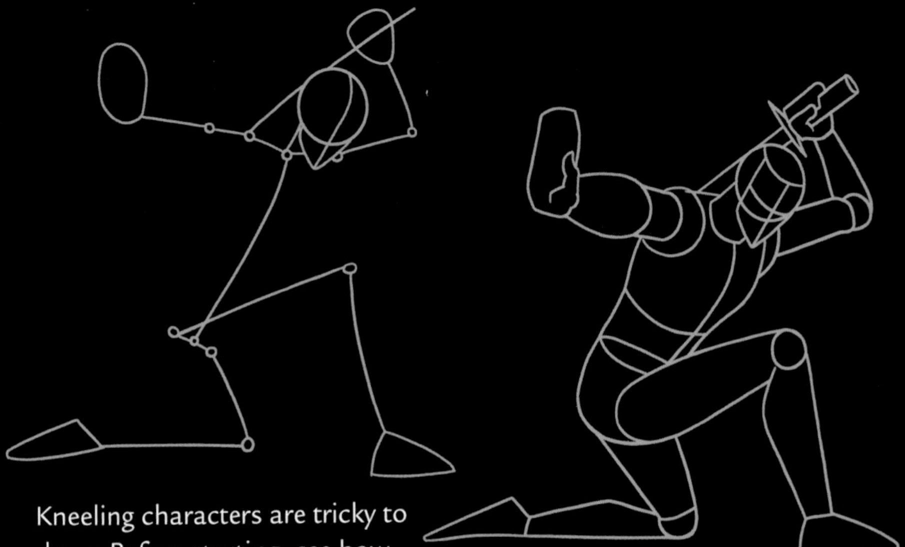

Kneeling characters are tricky to draw. Before starting, see how different body parts overlap.

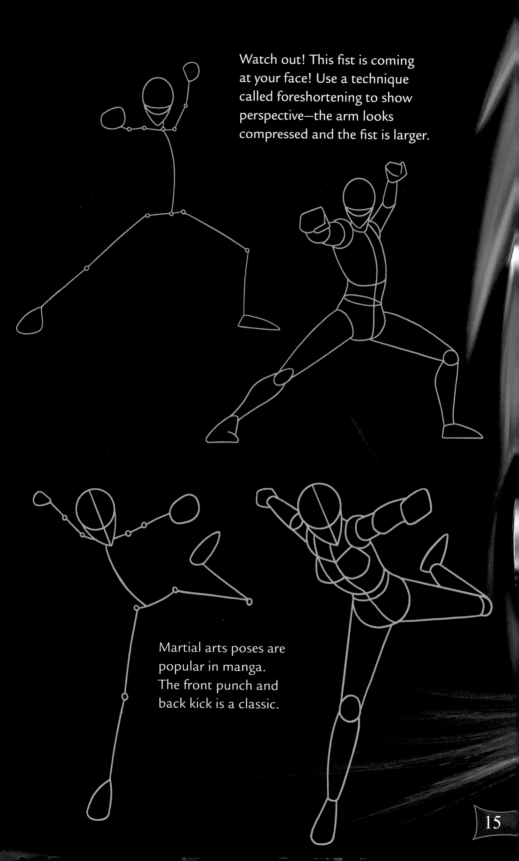

Watch out! This fist is coming at your face! Use a technique called foreshortening to show perspective—the arm looks compressed and the fist is larger.

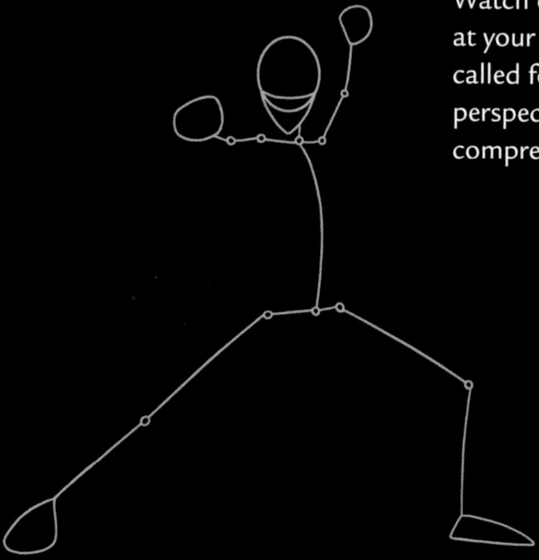

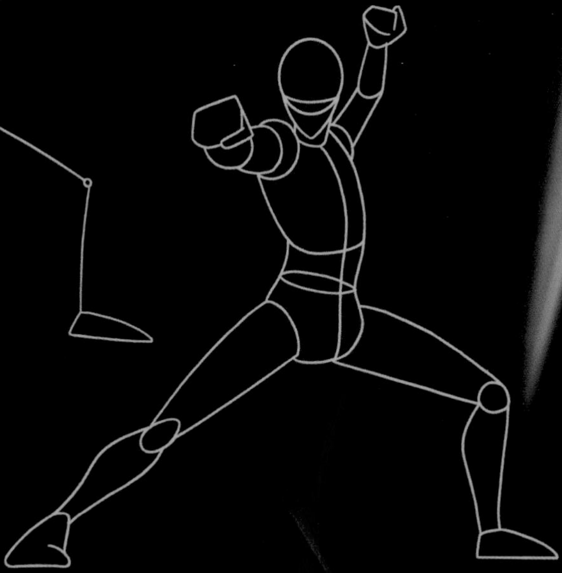

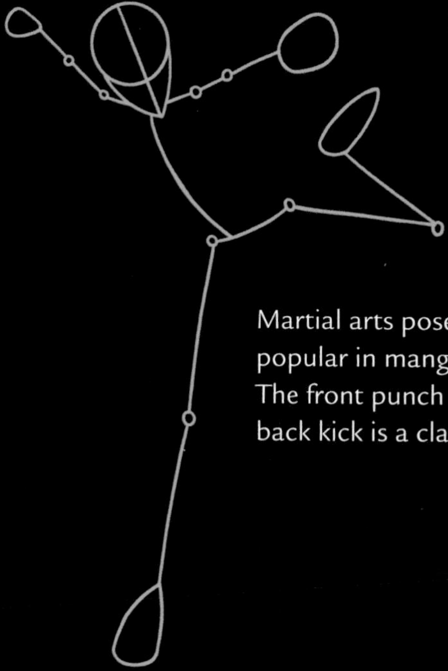

Martial arts poses are popular in manga. The front punch and back kick is a classic.

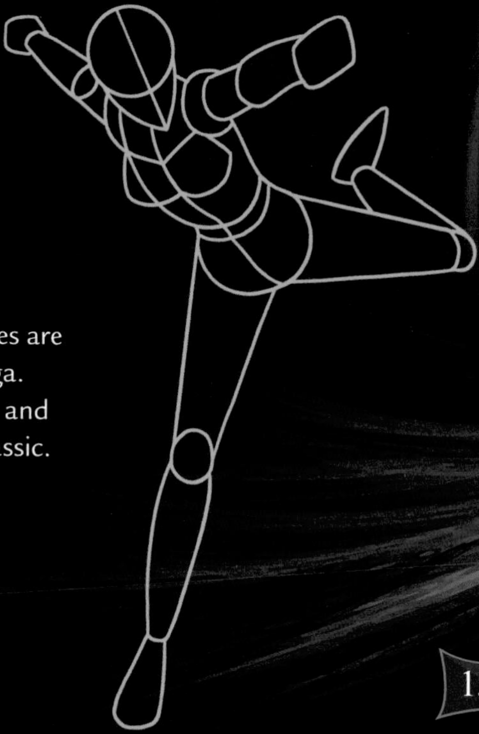

Chapter 4

# Details, Details

**Make your drawings come to life with costumes, accessories, and smart shading. Get creative!**

## Wardrobe Basics

Clothes make the man—and manga! Outfits and accessories make an instant statement about different types of characters, so get ready to play fashion designer.

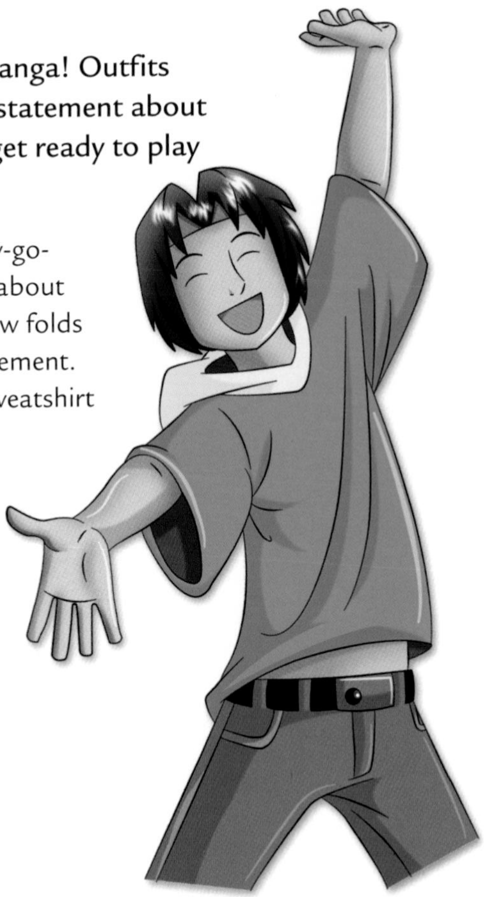

1 **Everyday outfits:** Young, happy-go-lucky characters like to lounge about in jeans and loose T-shirts. Draw folds and creases where there is movement. Folds are loose on the baggy sweatshirt but tighter on the jeans.

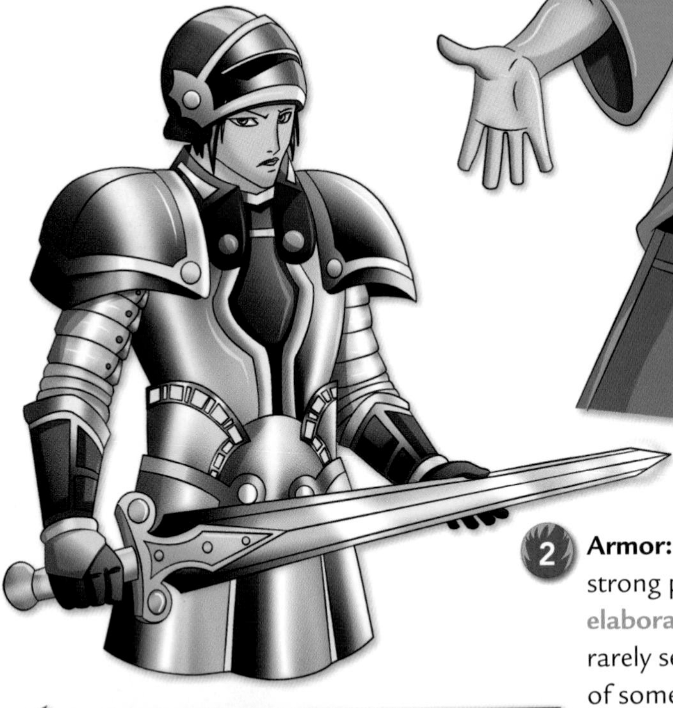

2 **Armor:** Warriors are fond of strong protective gear and elaborate belts. They are rarely seen without a weapon of some sort.



**elaborate:** with lots of details and decorations

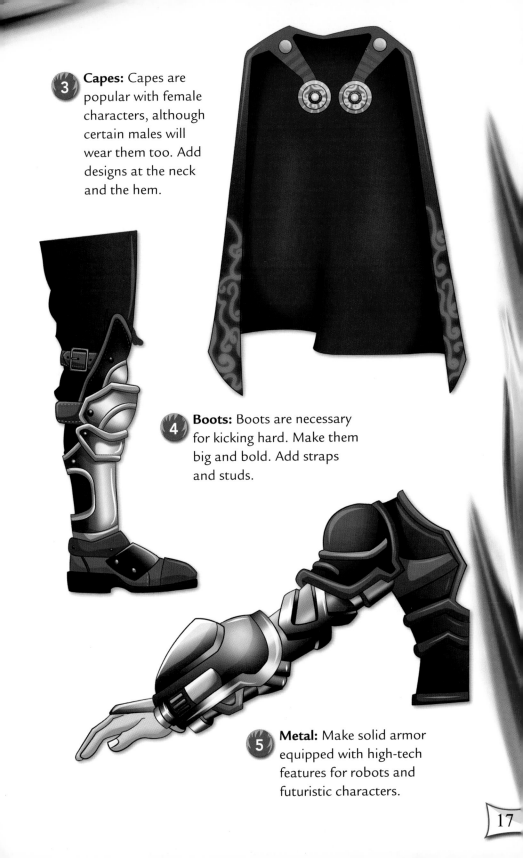

3 **Capes:** Capes are popular with female characters, although certain males will wear them too. Add designs at the neck and the hem.

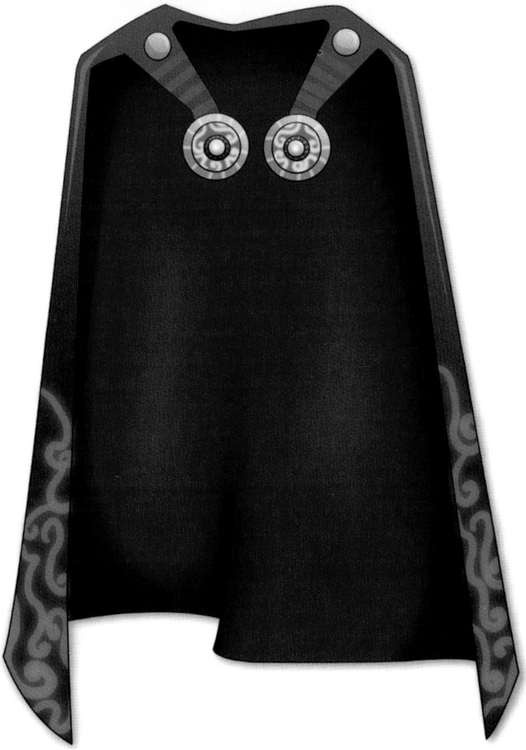

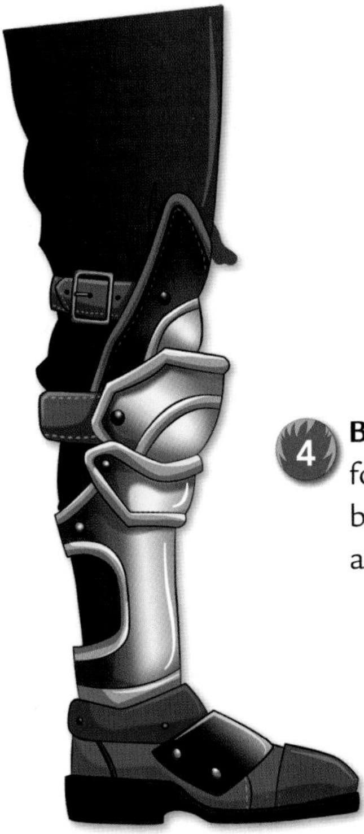

4 **Boots:** Boots are necessary for kicking hard. Make them big and bold. Add straps and studs.

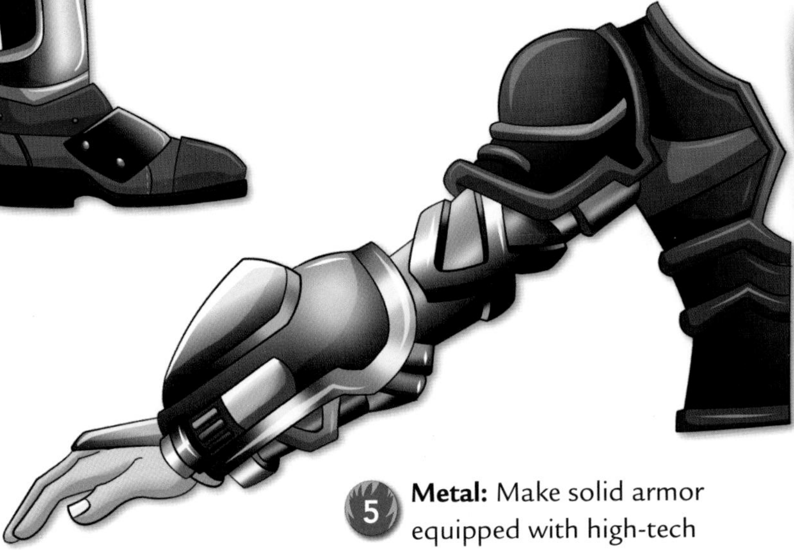

5 **Metal:** Make solid armor equipped with high-tech features for robots and futuristic characters.

# shading

You can work magic with black, white, and gray. Shading is key to adding depth to your drawings and giving them a three-dimensional look. It also helps add texture.

## Light and Shadows

Imagine a light source—like the bulb shown here—before you begin shading. The part of an object that the light hits stays white, while the rest is shadowed. Do you notice how the same light source illuminates different shapes differently?

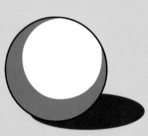

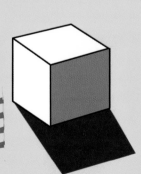

## Tips

- Shadows vary according to the shape of the object and the placement of the light source.
- Start shading about halfway down the object. Note that this rule changes for cubes and spheres.
- You can shade with color too. Just use lighter or darker hues of the same basic color.

**illuminate:** to light up, or make bright with light

Try to catch the play of shadows and light on your character's body and clothes.

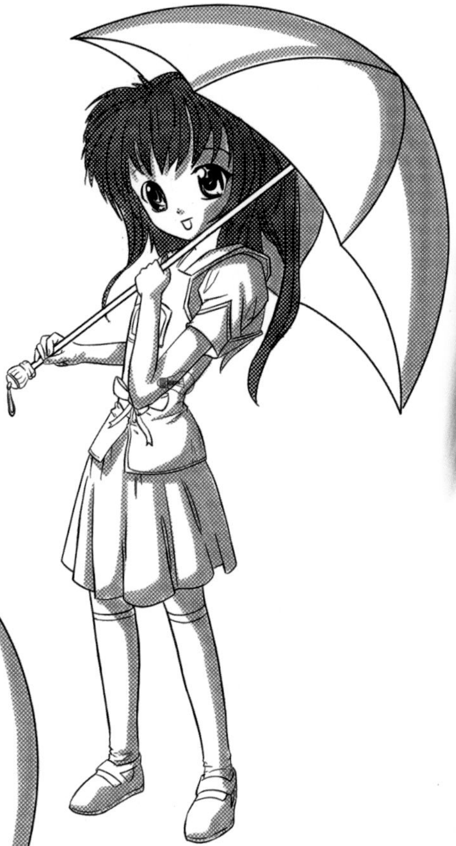

1 When the light shines from one side, the parts of the body facing the source appear bright. The parts facing away will be in shadow.

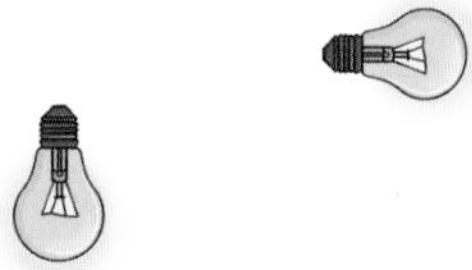

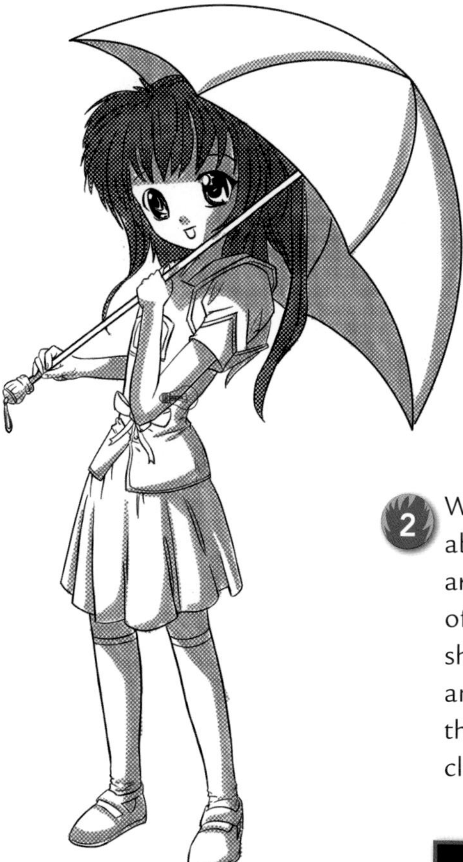

2 When the light falls from above, the exposed surfaces are illuminated. The inside of the umbrella is dark so a shadow is cast over the head and shoulders. Pay attention to the contours of the body and clothes as you shade.

**contour:** the outline of a shape or object

**Chapter 5**

# HEROES AND HEROINES

The heroes and heroines of manga comics have several features in common. They are tall, slender, good-looking, and have large eyes that indicate their honest nature.

## Traditional Hero

Dragons tremble and ladies grow weak in the knees when this dashing warrior arrives.

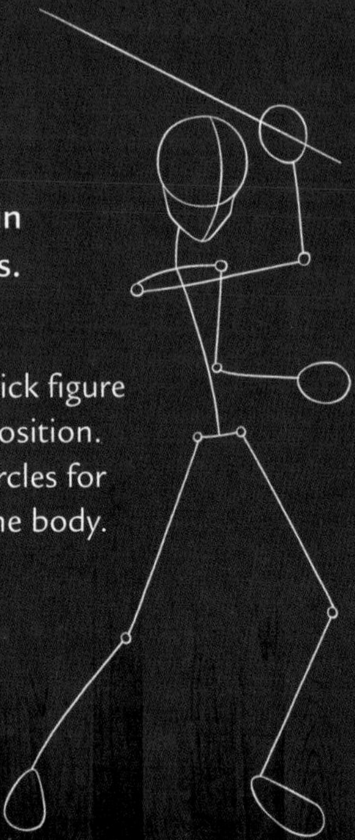

**1** Start with a stick figure in an action position. Make small circles for the joints in the body.

**2** Flesh out the body with curved lines and draw bigger circles for the kneecaps and elbow. Outline the sword.

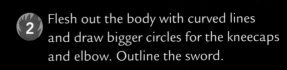

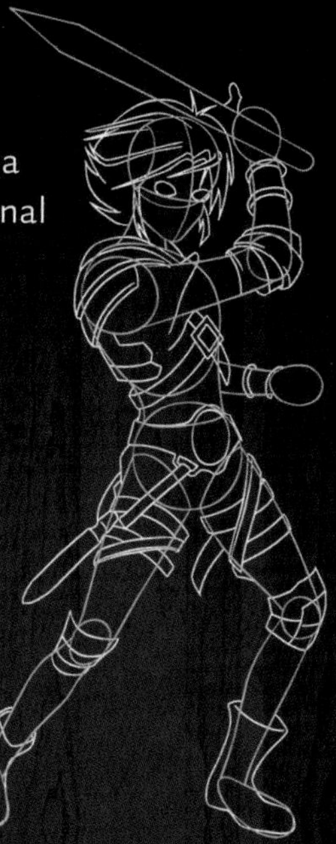

3  Armor, a large belt, boots, and a dagger are a must for a traditional hero. Add details to the face.

4  Add details to the clothes, weapons, and accessories. Mark the folds and creases that appear on his clothes as he gets ready to strike. Complete the face. Once your final sketch is ready, rub out any remaining guidelines.

# Tip

Use hard number-three pencils to make the first two stages of the drawing, since these are easier to erase. Use number-one or number-two pencils to sketch the final outline.

5  Color your hero. Clothes and accessories in green, gray, and brown give the warrior a military look. Draw a simple background. Some moonlight will add lots of drama. Make sure the sword glints.

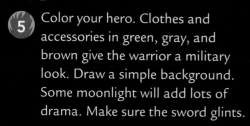

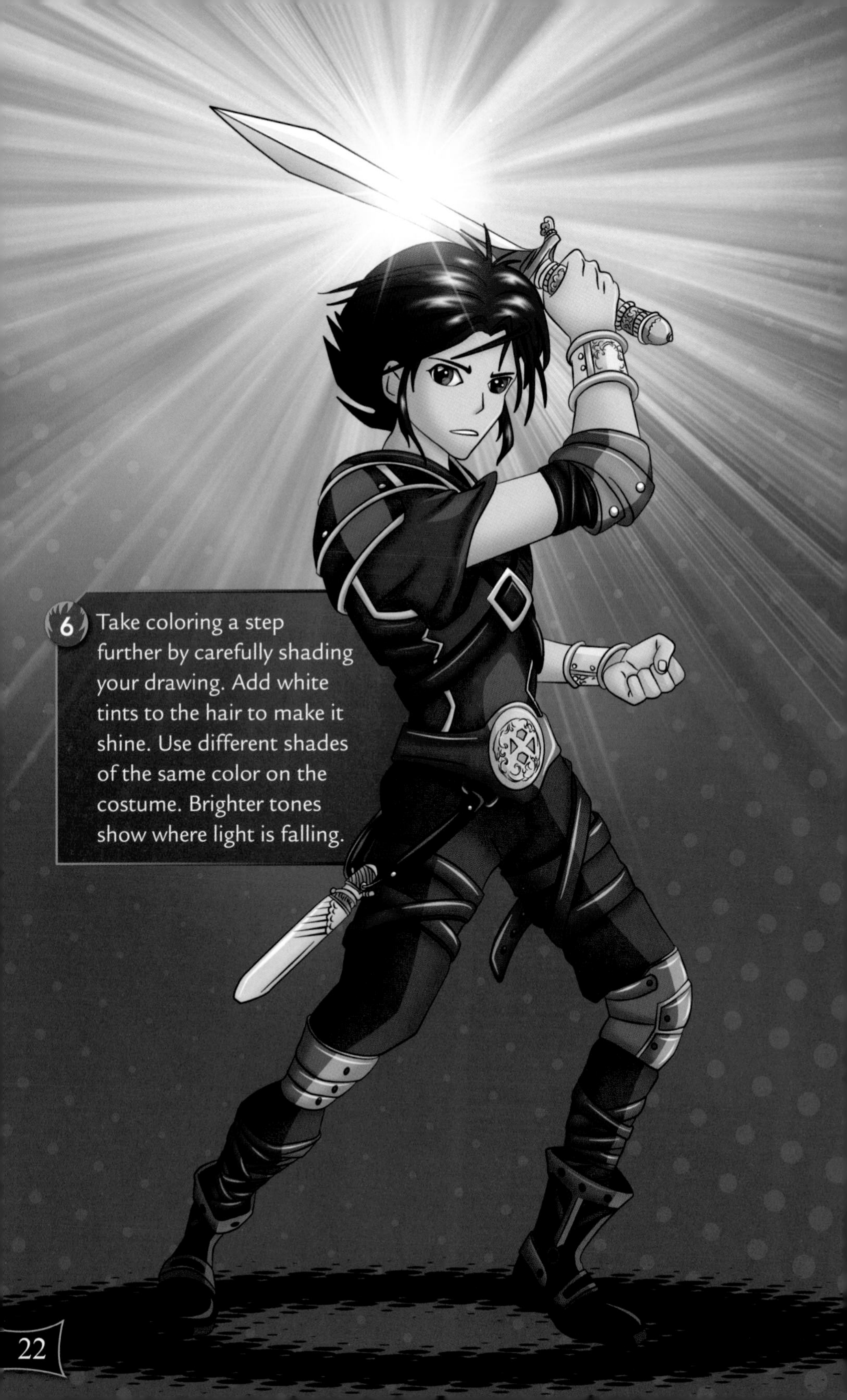

6 Take coloring a step further by carefully shading your drawing. Add white tints to the hair to make it shine. Use different shades of the same color on the costume. Brighter tones show where light is falling.

# Modern Warrior

With guns and eyes blazing, the modern warrior is a **formidable** foe. He can be quite sneaky sometimes, but he always does the right thing in the end.

1 Draw a stick figure. The warrior is crouching slightly, ready to shoot. Let the spine curve downward.

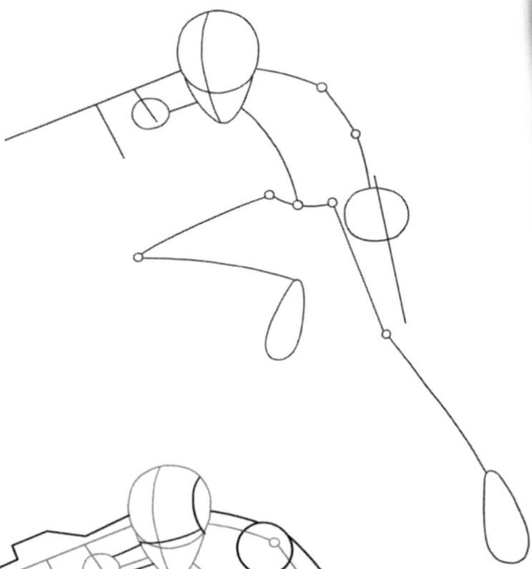

## Tip

Give your warrior a pointed chin and narrower eyes. The leaner and meaner he is, the more exaggerated these features should be.

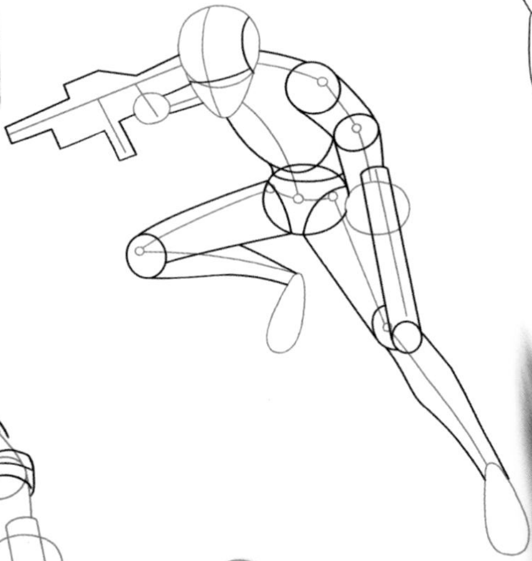

2 Give bulk to the warrior. Draw a circle for the hips, letting it overlap the waist and thighs. Flesh out the limbs.

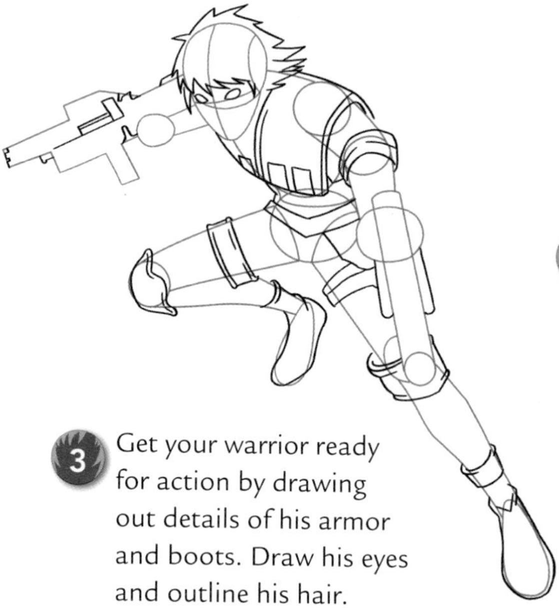

3 Get your warrior ready for action by drawing out details of his armor and boots. Draw his eyes and outline his hair.

**formidable:** powerful, inspires fear

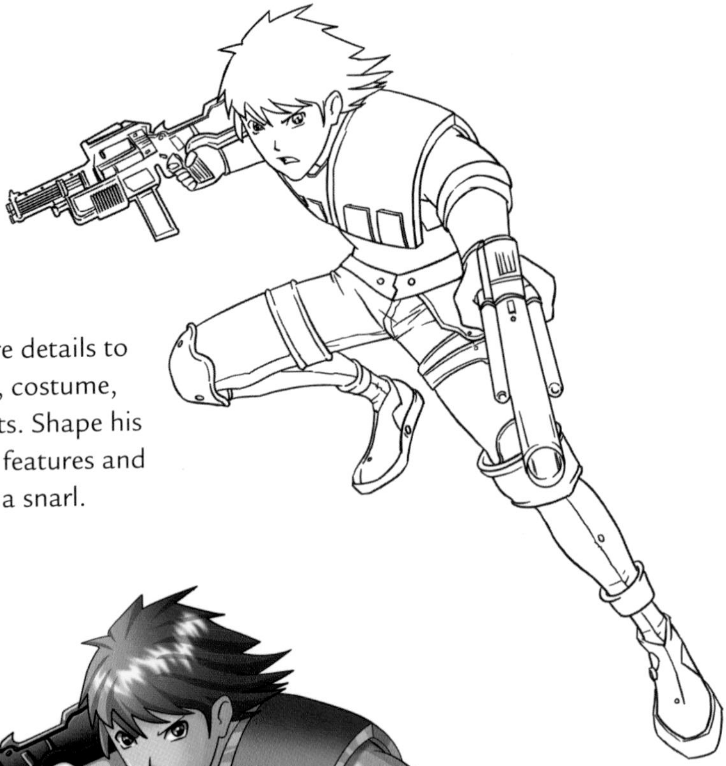

4 Add more details to the guns, costume, and boots. Shape his hair and features and give him a snarl.

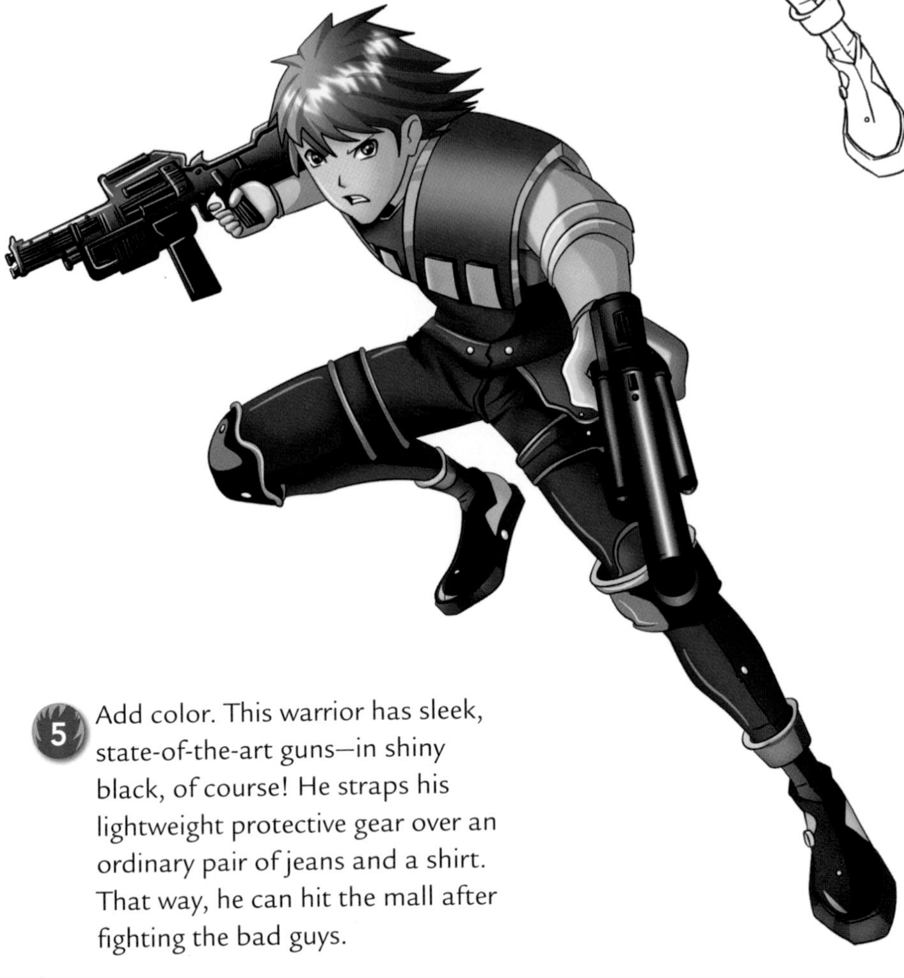

5 Add color. This warrior has sleek, state-of-the-art guns—in shiny black, of course! He straps his lightweight protective gear over an ordinary pair of jeans and a shirt. That way, he can hit the mall after fighting the bad guys.

# Warrior Princess

Warrior heroines are a force to reckon with! These combat queens have a softer side too. You can see it in their flowing locks and stylish accessories!

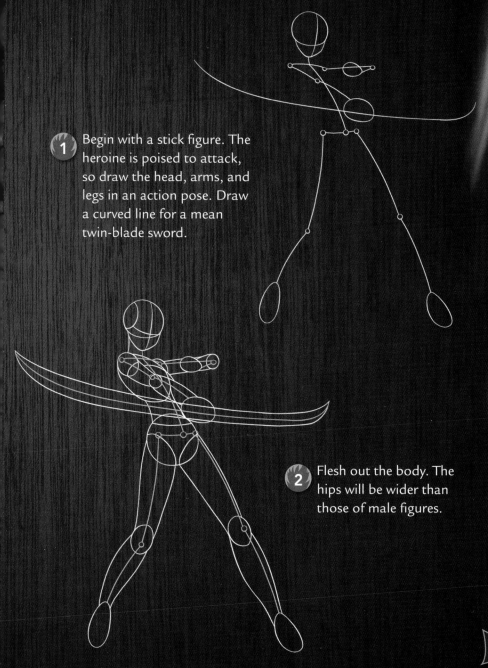

**1** Begin with a stick figure. The heroine is poised to attack, so draw the head, arms, and legs in an action pose. Draw a curved line for a mean twin-blade sword.

**2** Flesh out the body. The hips will be wider than those of male figures.

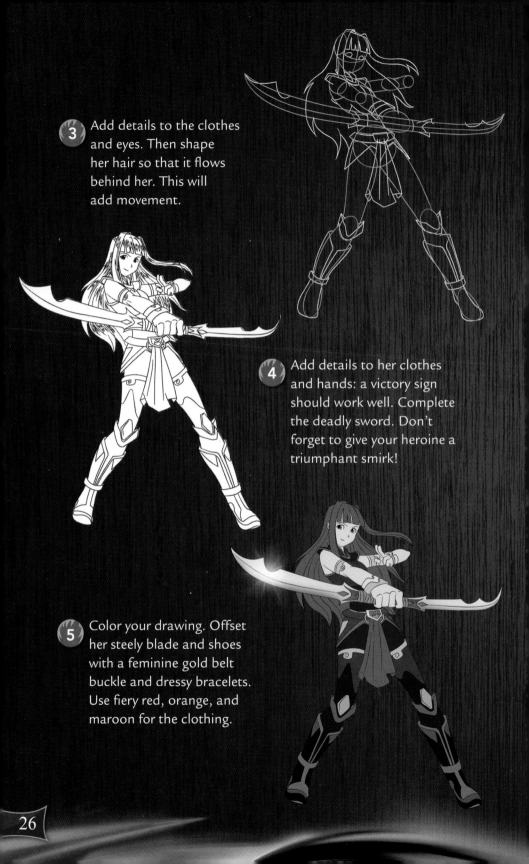

3 Add details to the clothes and eyes. Then shape her hair so that it flows behind her. This will add movement.

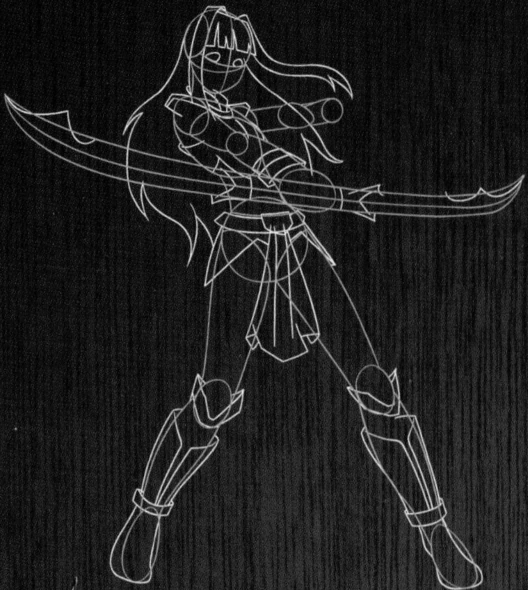

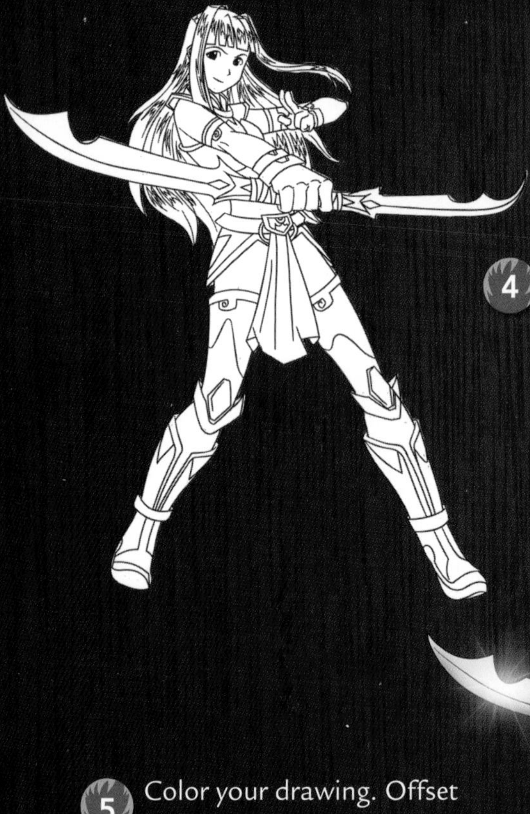

4 Add details to her clothes and hands: a victory sign should work well. Complete the deadly sword. Don’t forget to give your heroine a triumphant smirk!

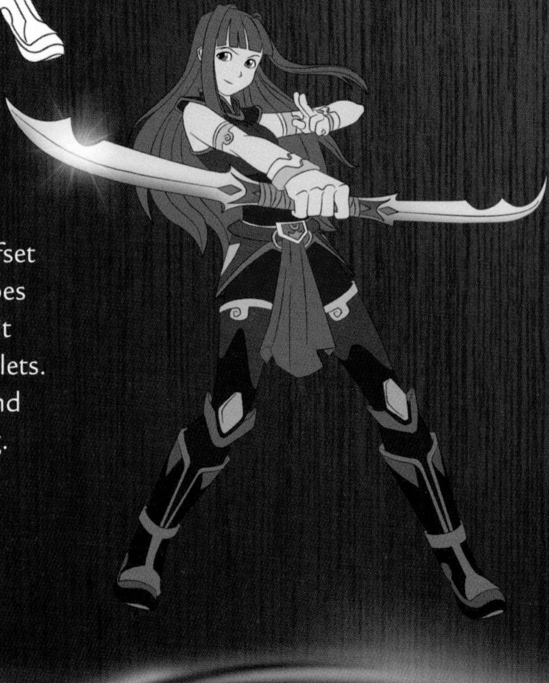

5 Color your drawing. Offset her steely blade and shoes with a feminine gold belt buckle and dressy bracelets. Use fiery red, orange, and maroon for the clothing.

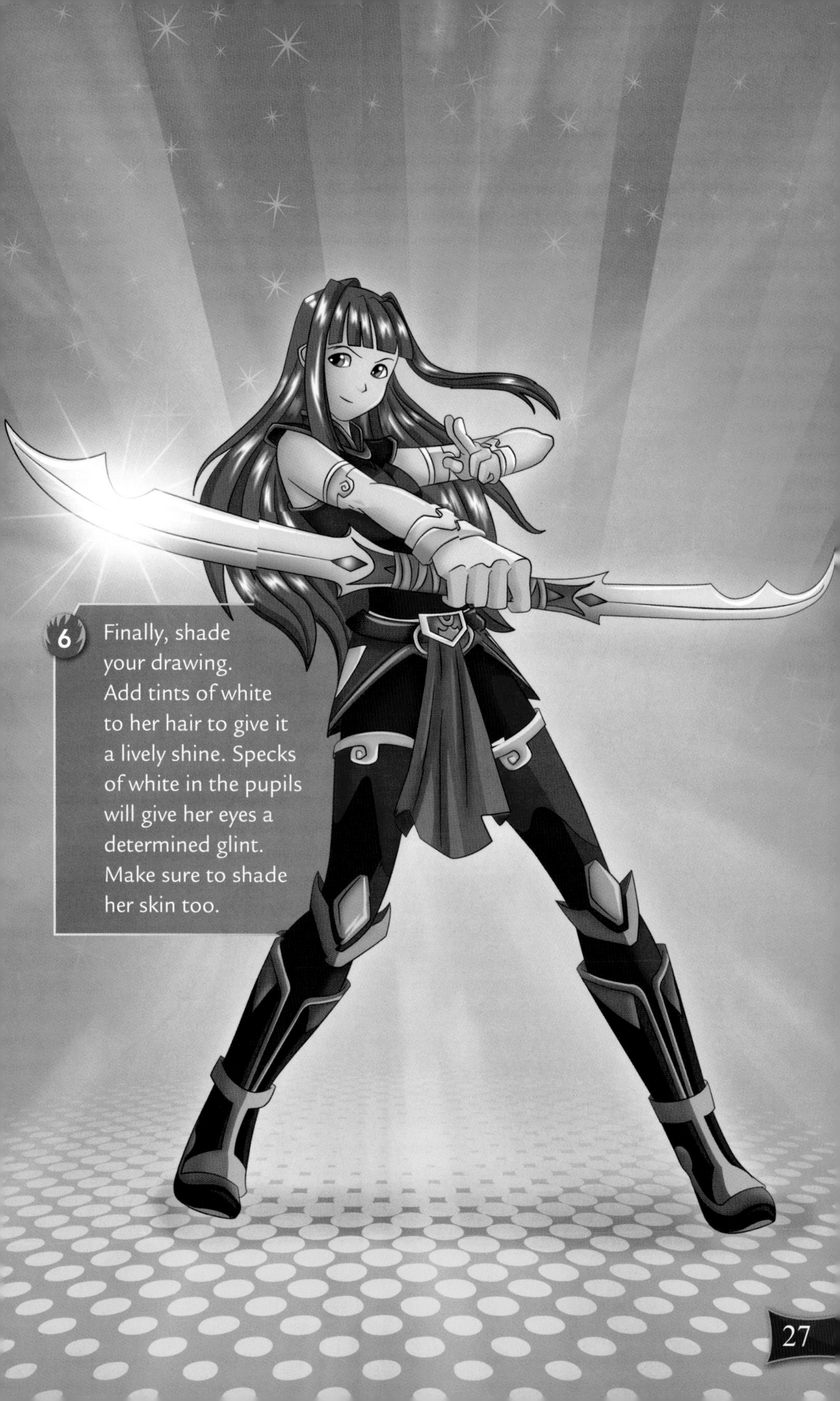

6 Finally, shade your drawing. Add tints of white to her hair to give it a lively shine. Specks of white in the pupils will give her eyes a determined glint. Make sure to shade her skin too.

# Modern Heroine

With her eyes always on target, this pistol-toting heroine means business. She's a bit of a tomboy and rarely lets her hair down.

**1** Your heroine has just burst into a room full of villains, so give the stick figure an aggressive pose. The hand facing you should be bigger than the other.

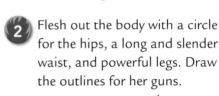

**2** Flesh out the body with a circle for the hips, a long and slender waist, and powerful legs. Draw the outlines for her guns.

**3** Dress her up in a flowing cloak, and let her hair fly in different directions. This will give movement to the character.

4 Add details to her face, hair, and body. Define her muscles. Mark out creases on the clothes.

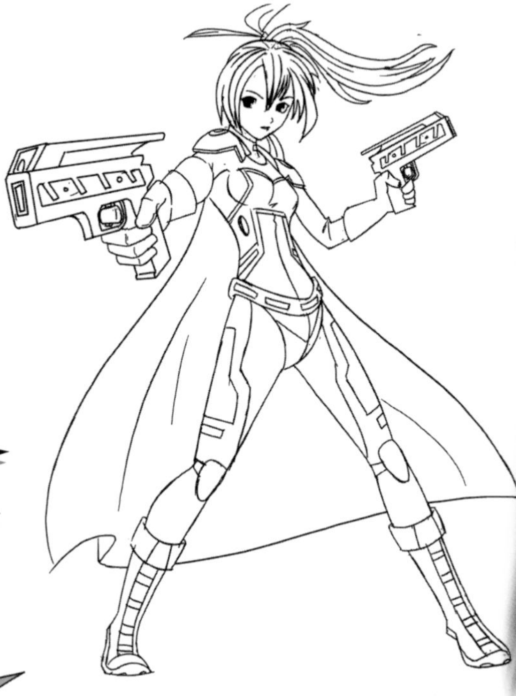

**Fact**

An entire genre of manga is devoted to "girls with guns."

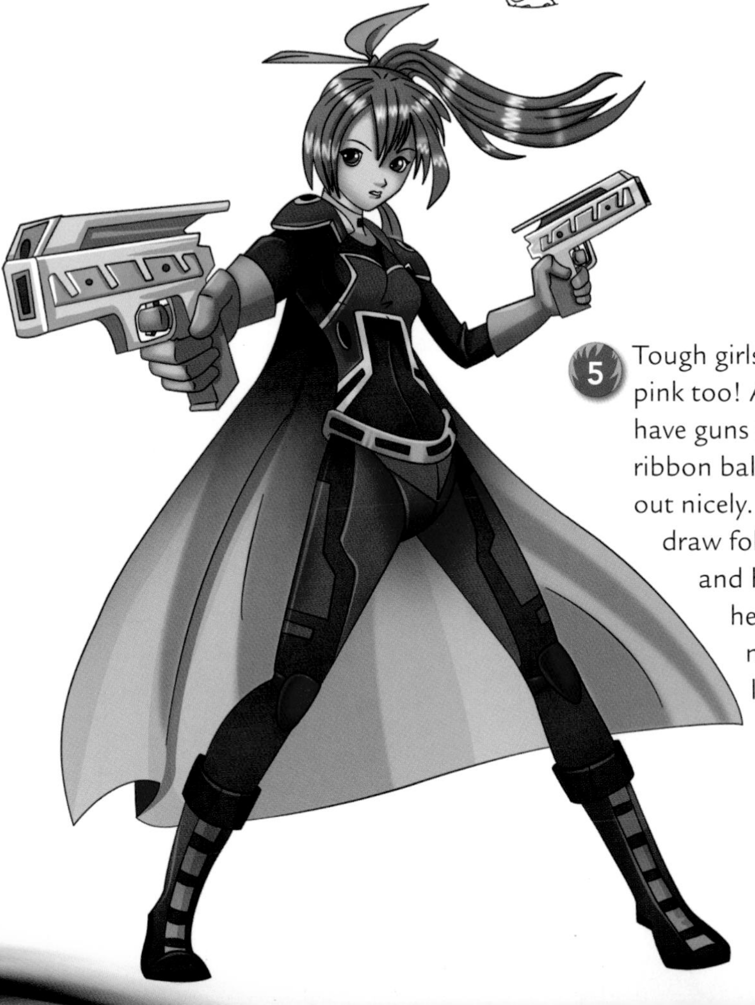

5 Tough girls can wear pink too! And when you have guns like that, a ribbon balances things out nicely. Make sure you draw folds in her cloak and highlights in her hair for a more realistic look.

# Chapter 6

# SPECIAL CHARACTERS

**The main protagonists are supported by a vast and varied cast of supporting characters.**

## Sensei

The sensei, or grandmaster, is no spring chicken, but he can run circles around the fiercest young fighters.

**1** Draw a stick figure in a fighting position, with legs apart and arms raised to the sides.

**2** Flesh out the stick figure. Remember, the sensei is a rather wiry fellow. Draw circles to define the joints.

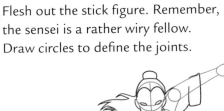

**3** Give your sensei a samurai-style hairdo. Make his wispy beard flow in the opposite direction. Dress him up in martial arts clothes.

**protagonist: the lead character of a story**

4 Add details to the hair and face. Don't forget the bushy eyebrows! Once your final outline is ready, rub out the guidelines.

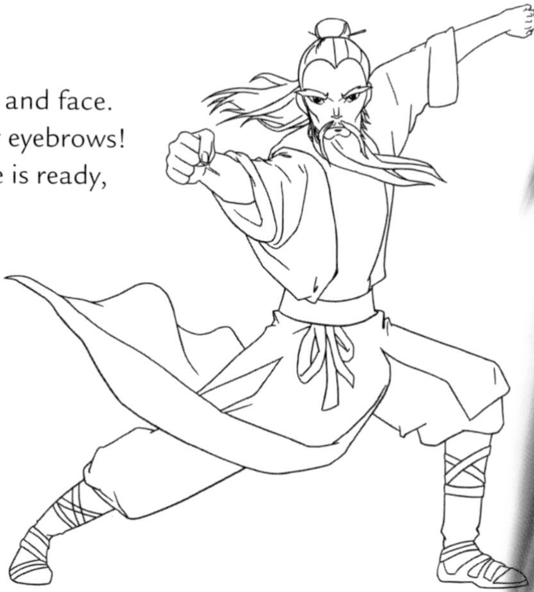

**Tip**

Older faces have more defined cheekbones and the eyes are deeper set.

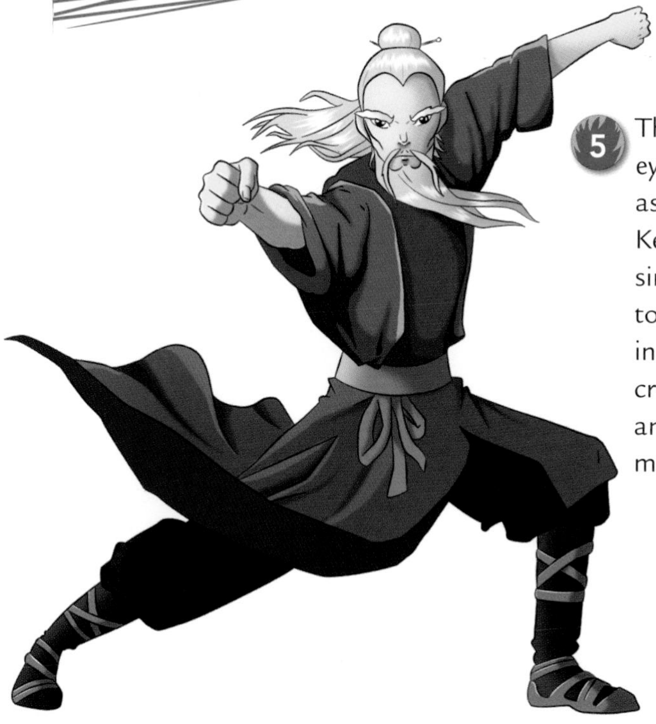

5 This old-timer's eyebrows are as gray as his hair and beard. Keep the colors simple, but be sure to bring out the folds in the clothes. The creases on the sleeves and tunic help add movement.

# Mecha

Mecha are robots with a human touch—they are piloted by people. They can squash everything in sight, shoot weapons, and even perform martial arts stunts.

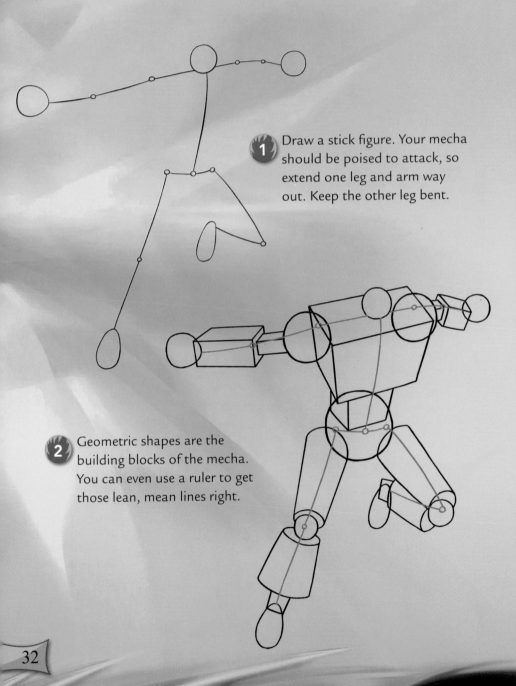

**1** Draw a stick figure. Your mecha should be poised to attack, so extend one leg and arm way out. Keep the other leg bent.

**2** Geometric shapes are the building blocks of the mecha. You can even use a ruler to get those lean, mean lines right.

3 No mecha is complete without some serious armor. Add thrusters at the back. Make sure the arms are pointed backward. This posture brings force to your drawing.

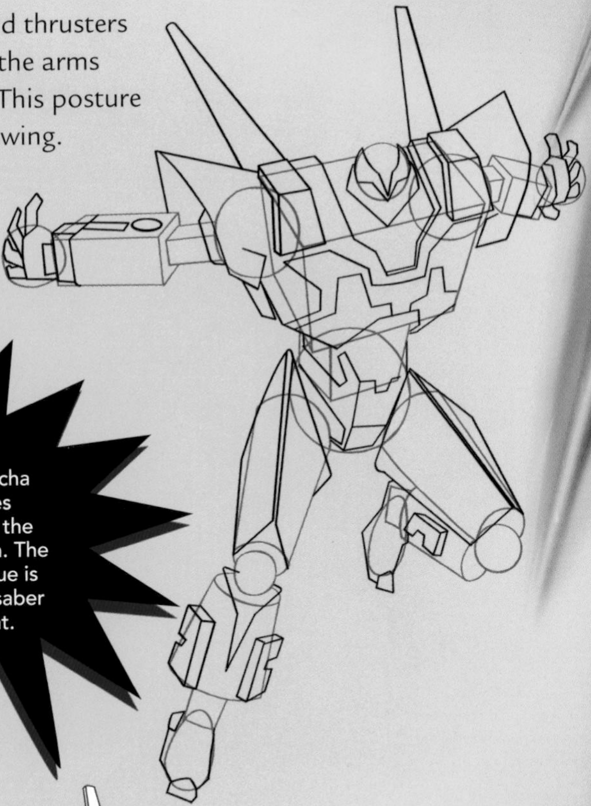

**Fact**

A giant statue of a mecha from the anime series *Gundam* watches over the city of Shizuoka in Japan. The 59-foot (18-meter) statue is equipped with a beam saber that lights up at night.

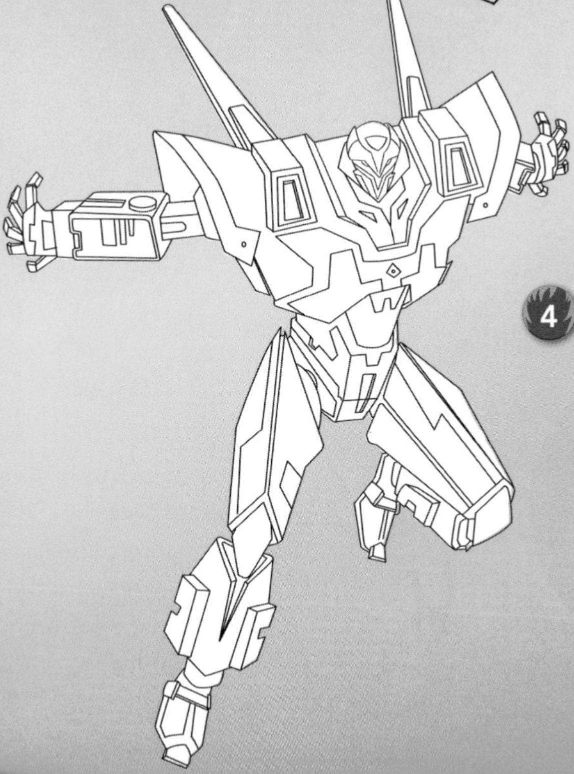

4 Add details to the mecha. You can go as high-tech as you want with the look.

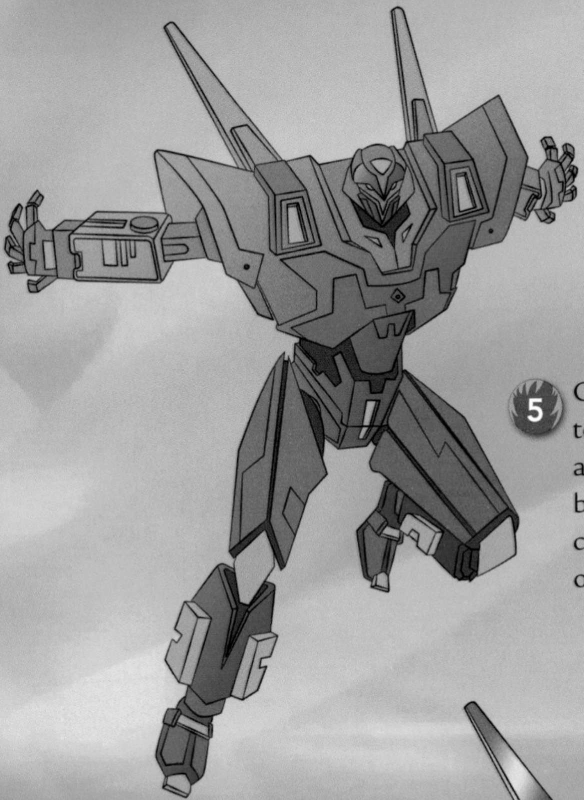

5 Color the mecha. Add touches of gray to give it a metallic appearance, but don't be afraid to use colors for different parts of his gear.

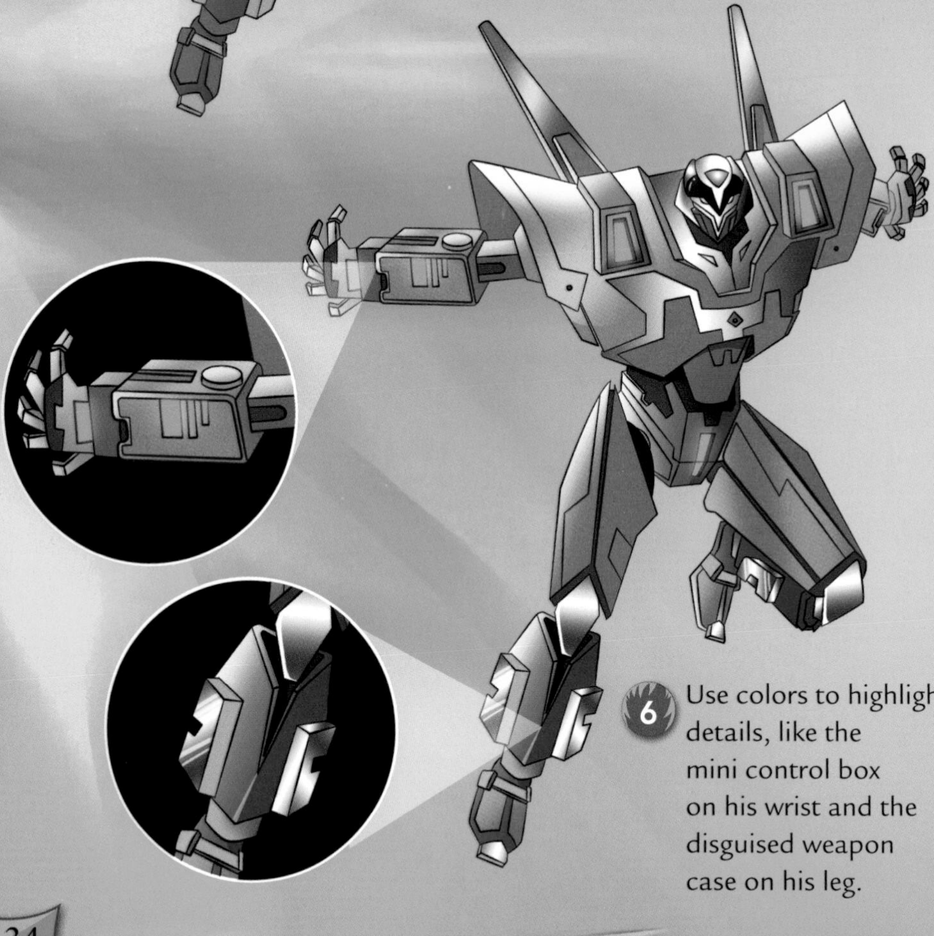

6 Use colors to highlight details, like the mini control box on his wrist and the disguised weapon case on his leg.

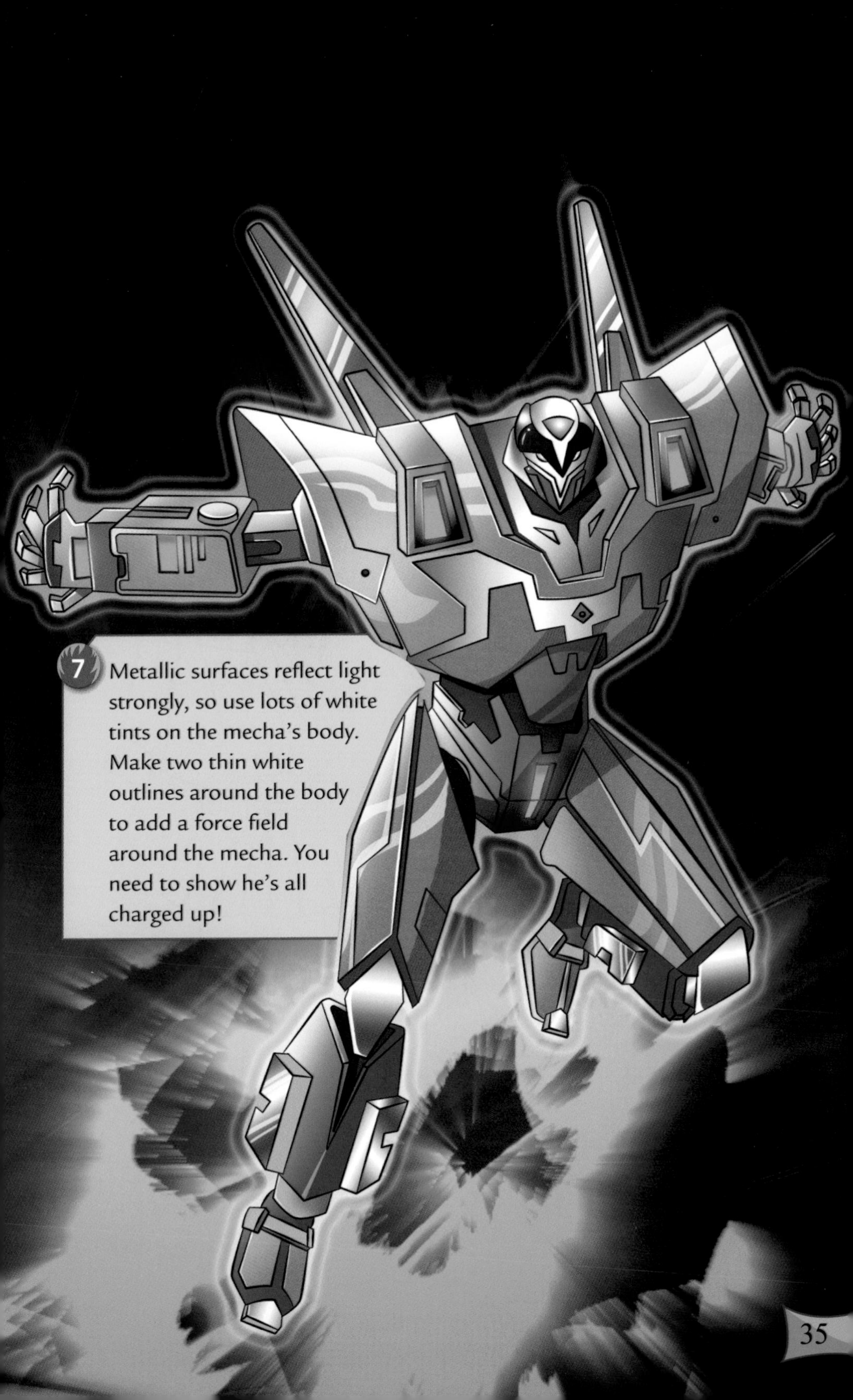

**7** Metallic surfaces reflect light strongly, so use lots of white tints on the mecha's body. Make two thin white outlines around the body to add a force field around the mecha. You need to show he's all charged up!

# Chibis

A chibi is a cute little creature with a large head and tiny body. The body, feet, and hands are very basic, but the eyes as well as the hair can be wild and expressive. Sometimes, normal characters transform into chibis for a short while. This happens when they feel extreme emotions.

## Tip

Chibi characters have a body-to-head **ratio** of about 1:1. A normal child's ratio is approximately 4:1.

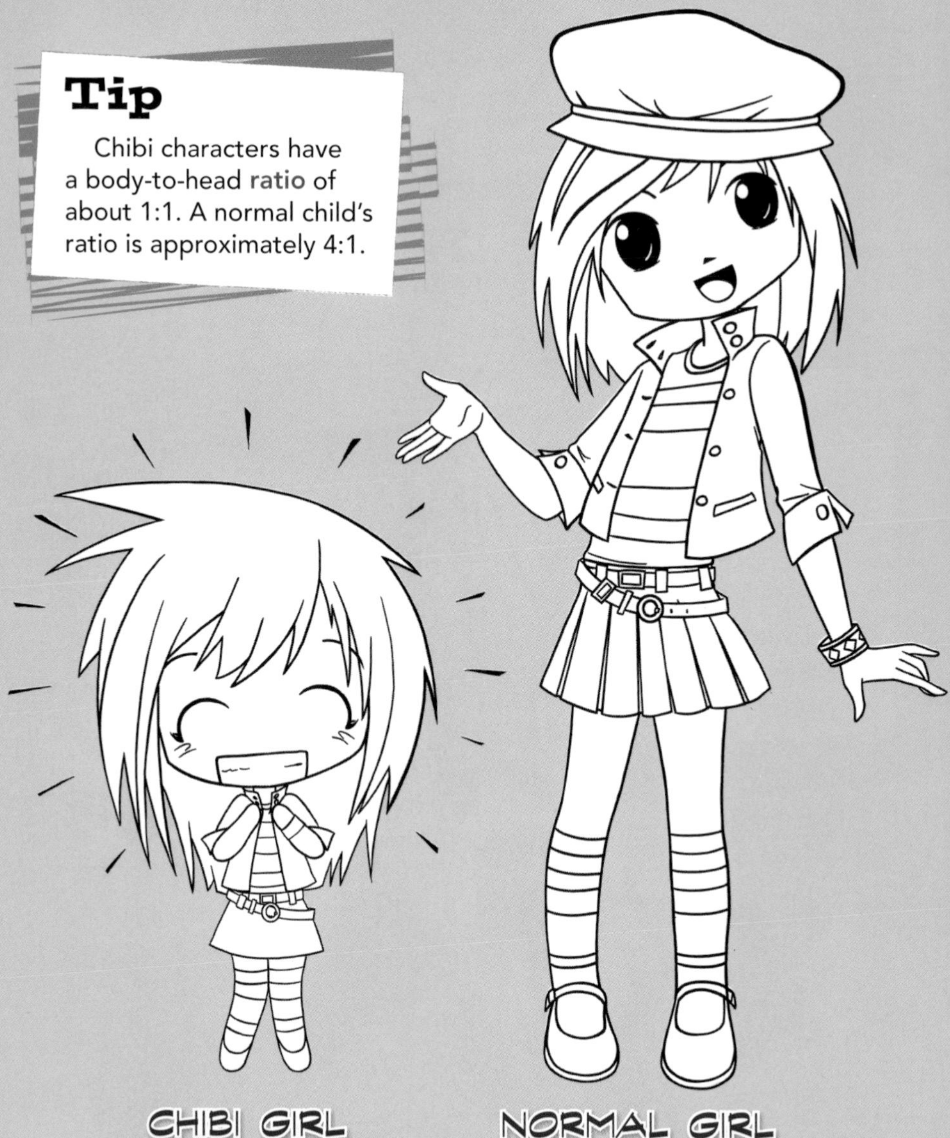
CHIBI GIRL
NORMAL GIRL



**ratio**: the number of times one quantity contains another similar quantity

A chibi's eyes take up most of its noseless face. They tell you all there is to know about the character.

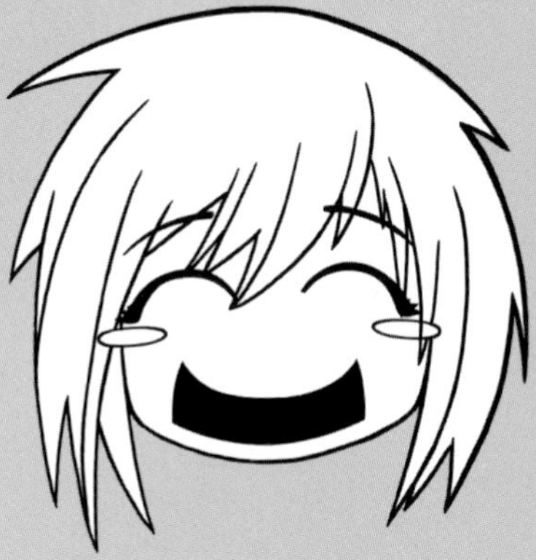

DELIGHTED

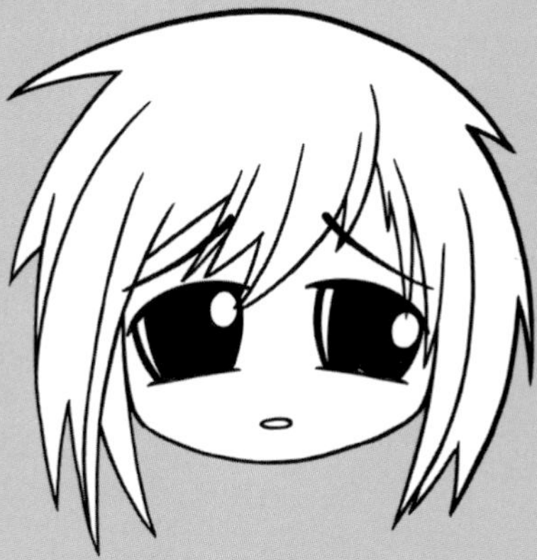

WORRIED

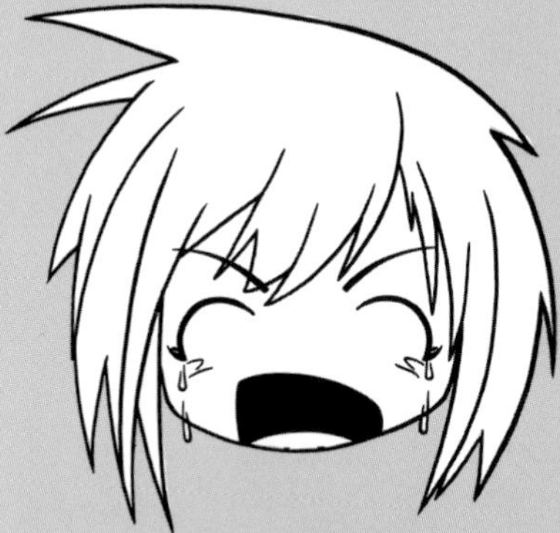

SAD

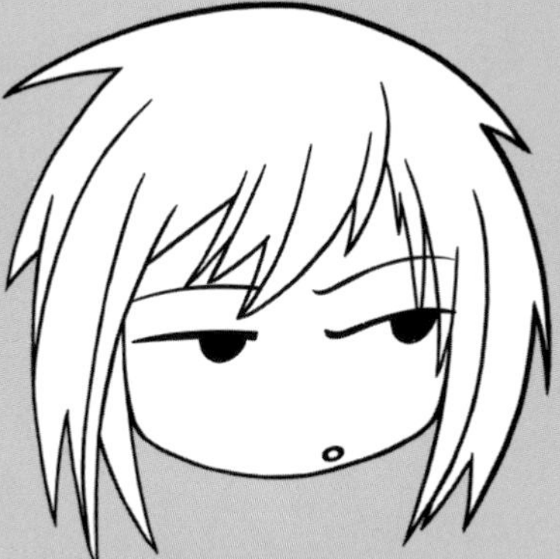

SNEAKY

**Fact**

A chibi causes lots of drama and excitement but its antics don't affect the main story.

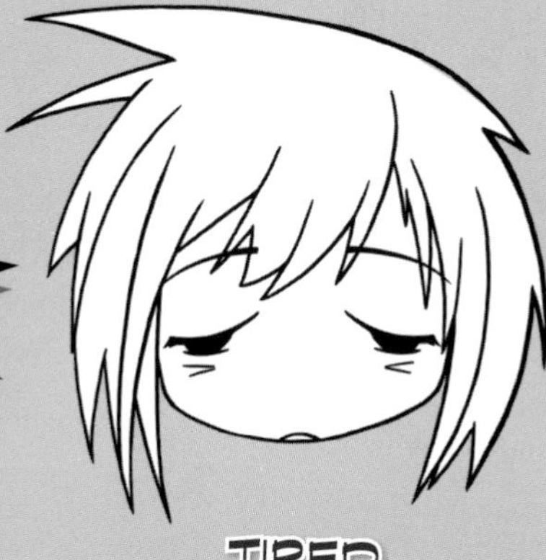

TIRED

# Magical Girl

She's cute but ordinary until one day—boom! She discovers she has special powers. These could range from being able to fly to casting magic spells.

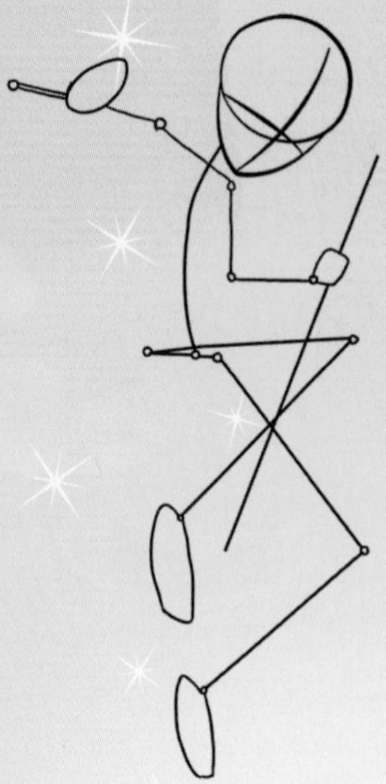

1 Draw a stick figure. This girl is flying, so her legs should be raised and bent.

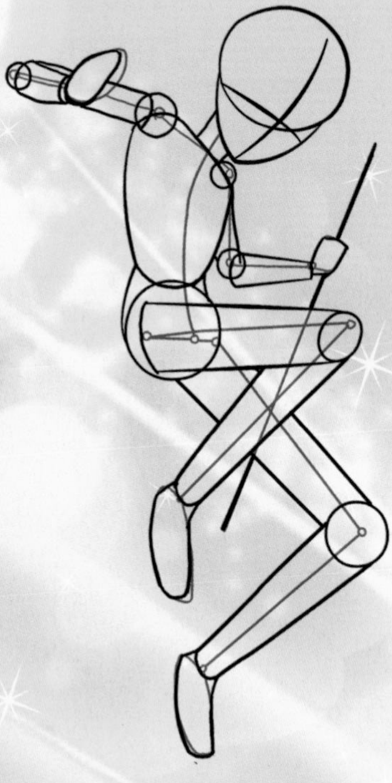

2 Flesh out the body. The circle to show the hip will be small since the girl still has a childish body shape.

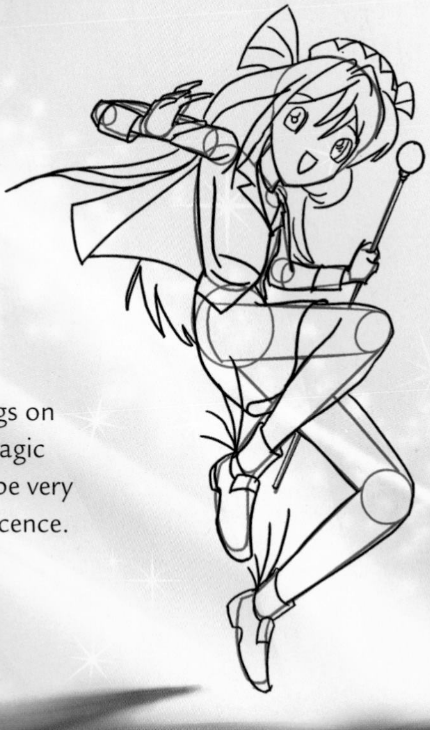

3 Add a magic cloak, wings on the shoes, and a cute magic wand. The eyes should be very round to show her innocence.

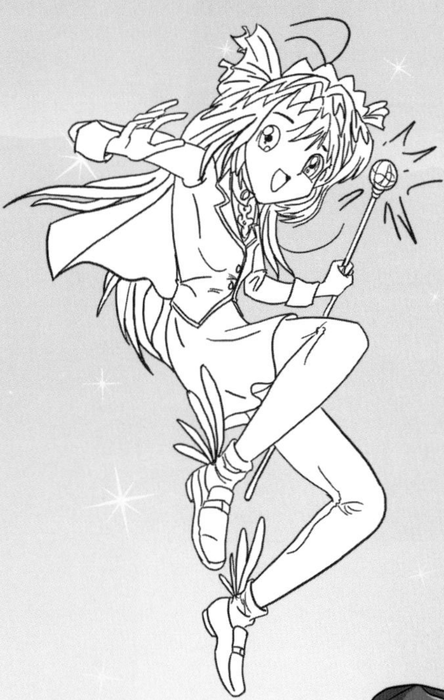

4 Add final details to the outfit and hair. She should look surprised but happy!

5 Finally, add color. Think bright and girly. Red hair with golden tints sets her apart from the crowd. Add a magical glow around the wand.

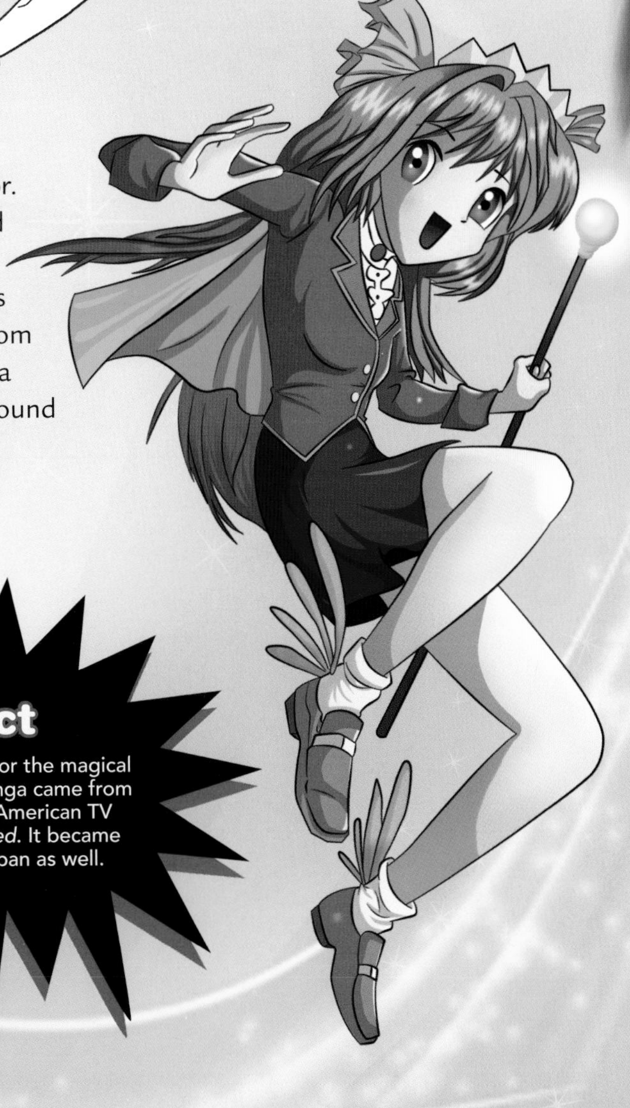

## Fact

The inspiration for the magical girl genre in manga came from the 1960s hit American TV series *Bewitched*. It became popular in Japan as well.

# THE BIG PICTURE

It's time to make a manga comic! Once you decide on your characters and story, make a storyboard. Then simply add details and words.

Arrange panels according to the scenes and situations you want to show. Make a rough sketch of your characters.

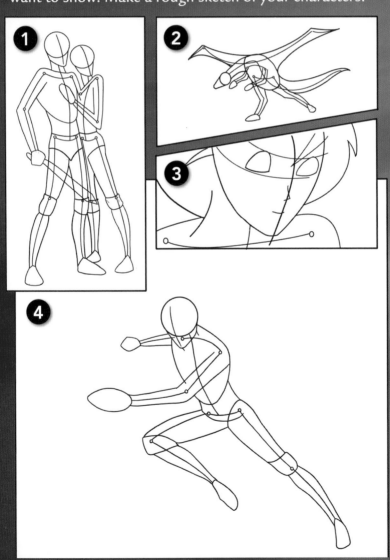

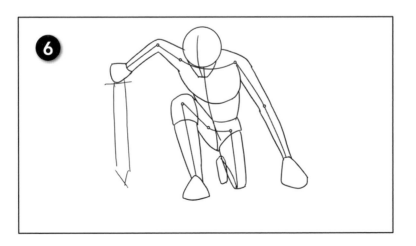

Flesh out your characters, adding details as you go along. Keep the background simple so that the focus stays on the characters. Fine lines around a character help show action and excitement.

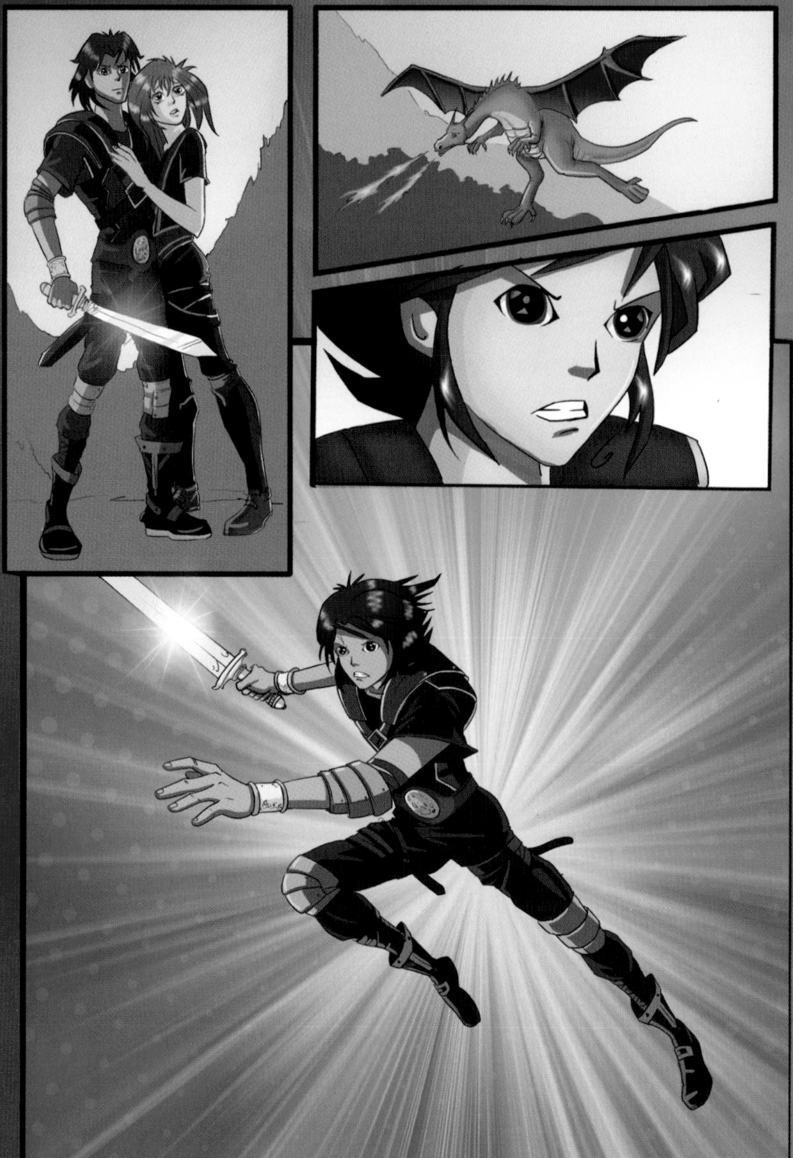

Add drama with color and shapes. The splashes of red on a black background represent the fight between the hero and the dragon. This adds drama and a more sophisticated look.

## Fact

In Japan, manga is read from right to left! This format is often followed in Western countries as well.

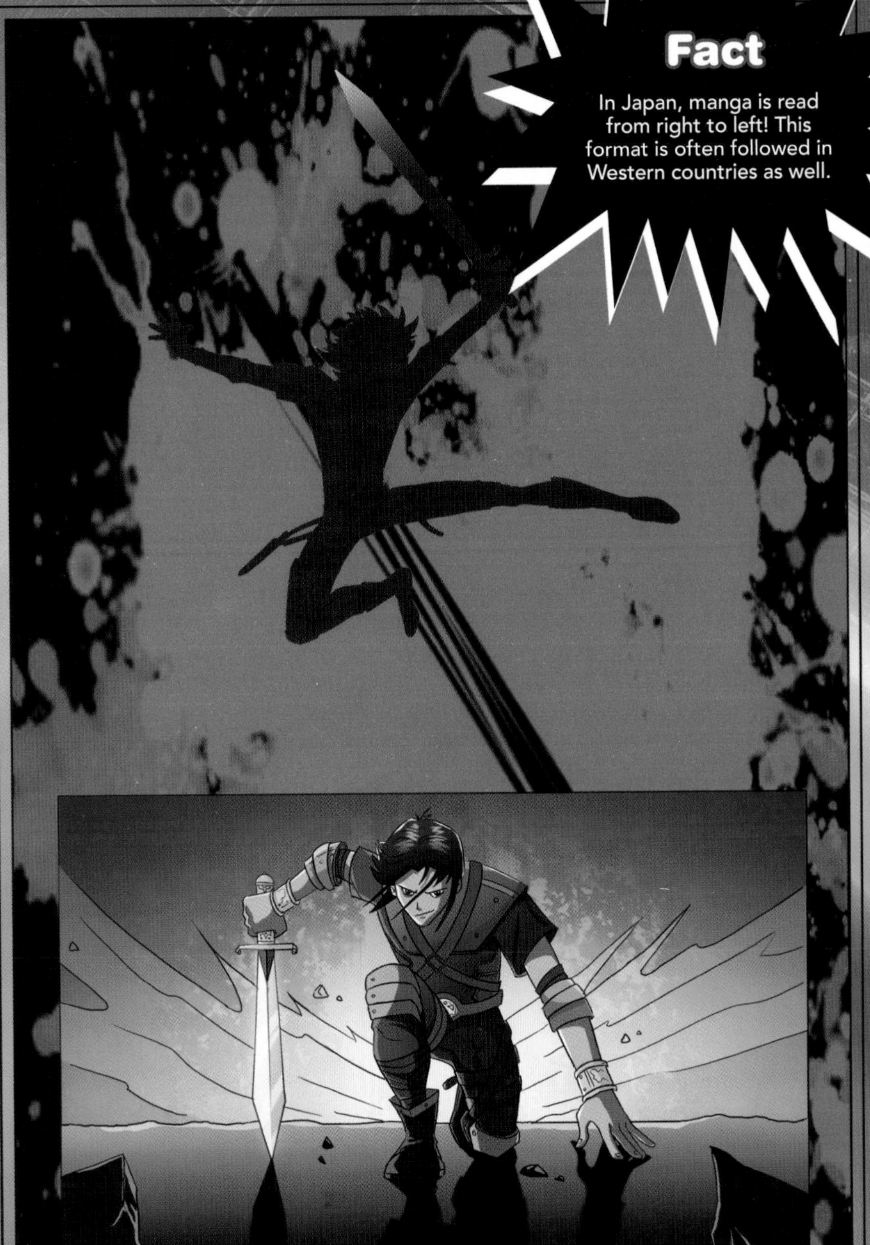

Use your imagination—and speech bubbles—to complete your story.

Zenada is the last princess of the Kagaza kingdom. All her six sisters have just been killed by Aagakha, the dragon. She runs into the forest and stumbles into the arms of outlaw-warrior Shomo.

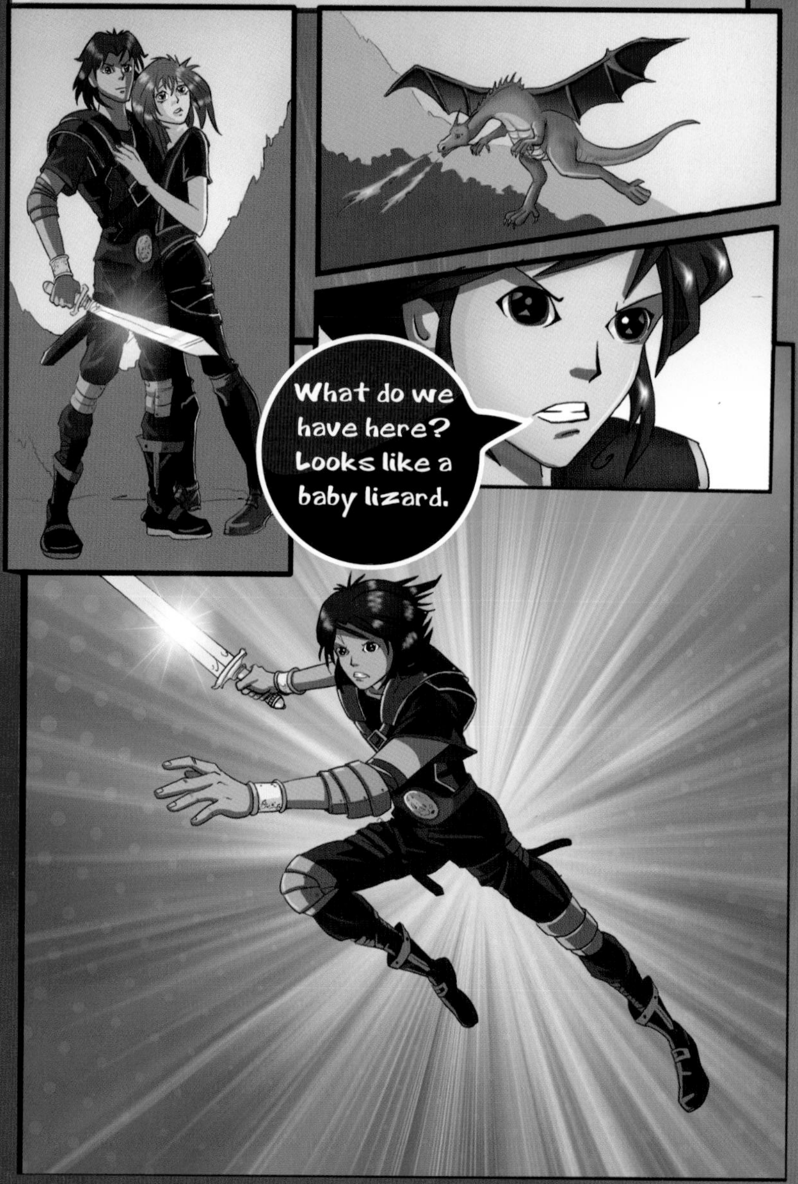
What do we have here? Looks like a baby lizard.

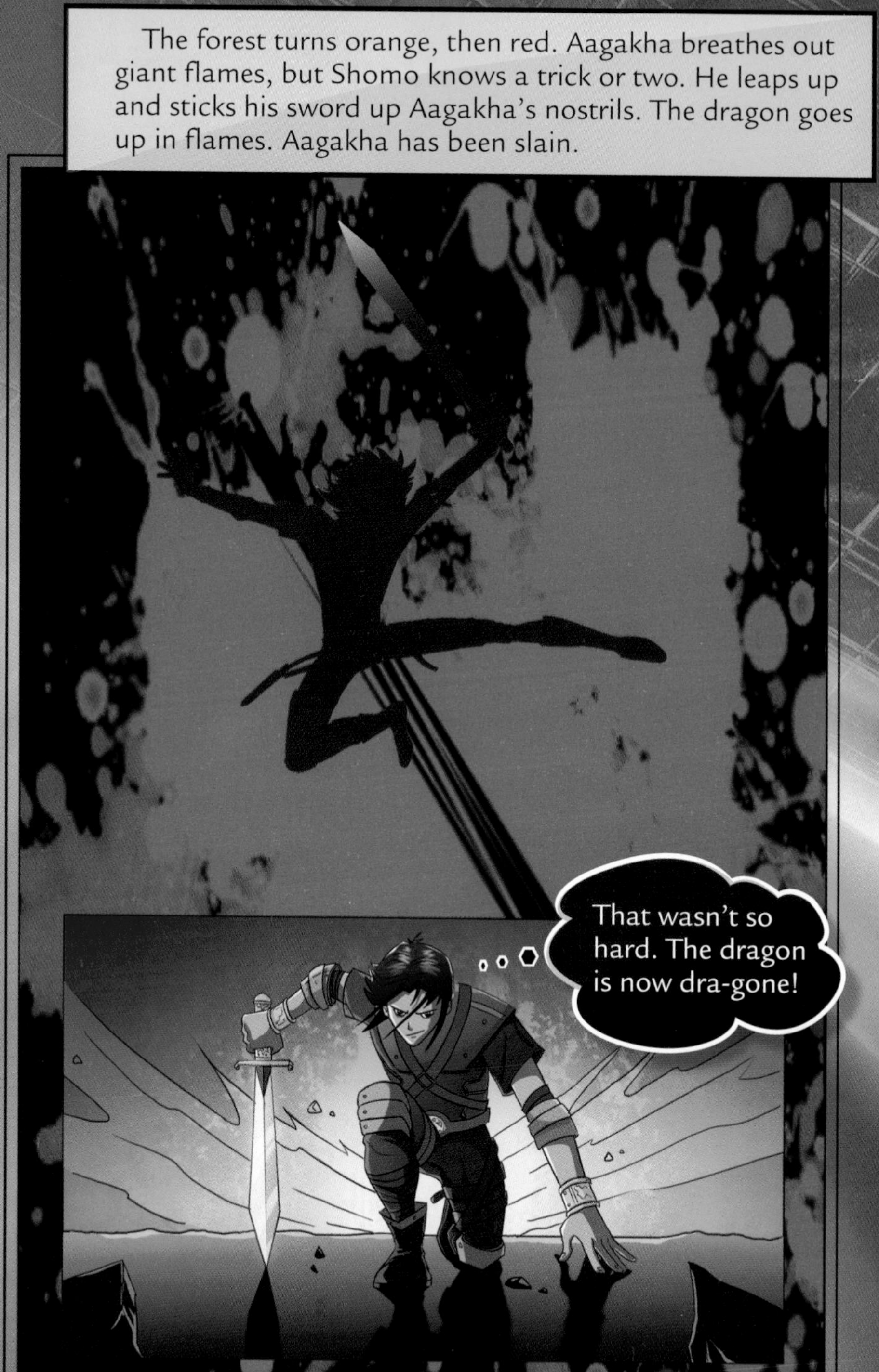
The forest turns orange, then red. Aagakha breathes out giant flames, but Shomo knows a trick or two. He leaps up and sticks his sword up Aagakha's nostrils. The dragon goes up in flames. Aagakha has been slain.
That wasn't so hard. The dragon is now dra-gone!

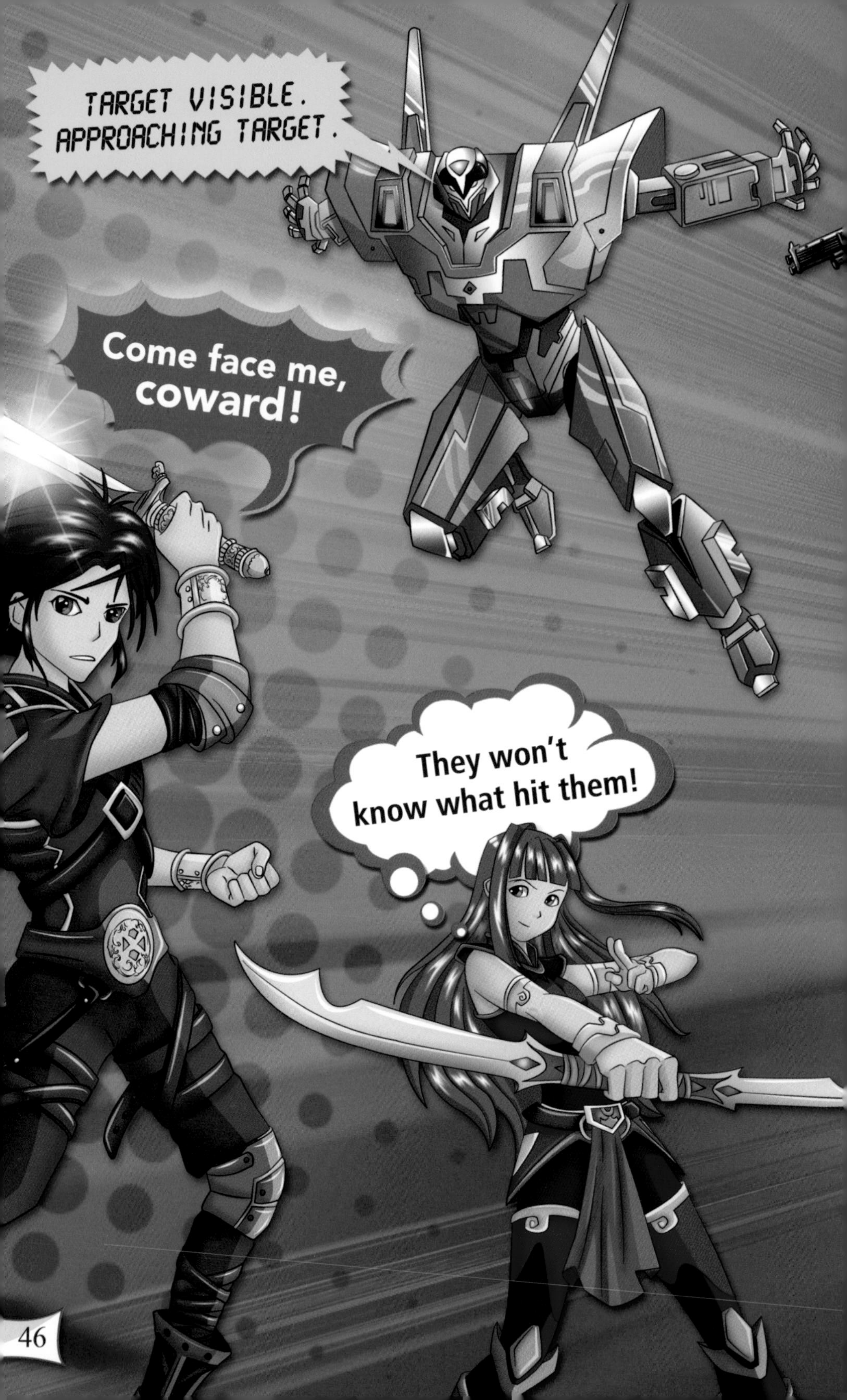
TARGET VISIBLE.
APPROACHING TARGET.
Come face me, coward!
They won't know what hit them!

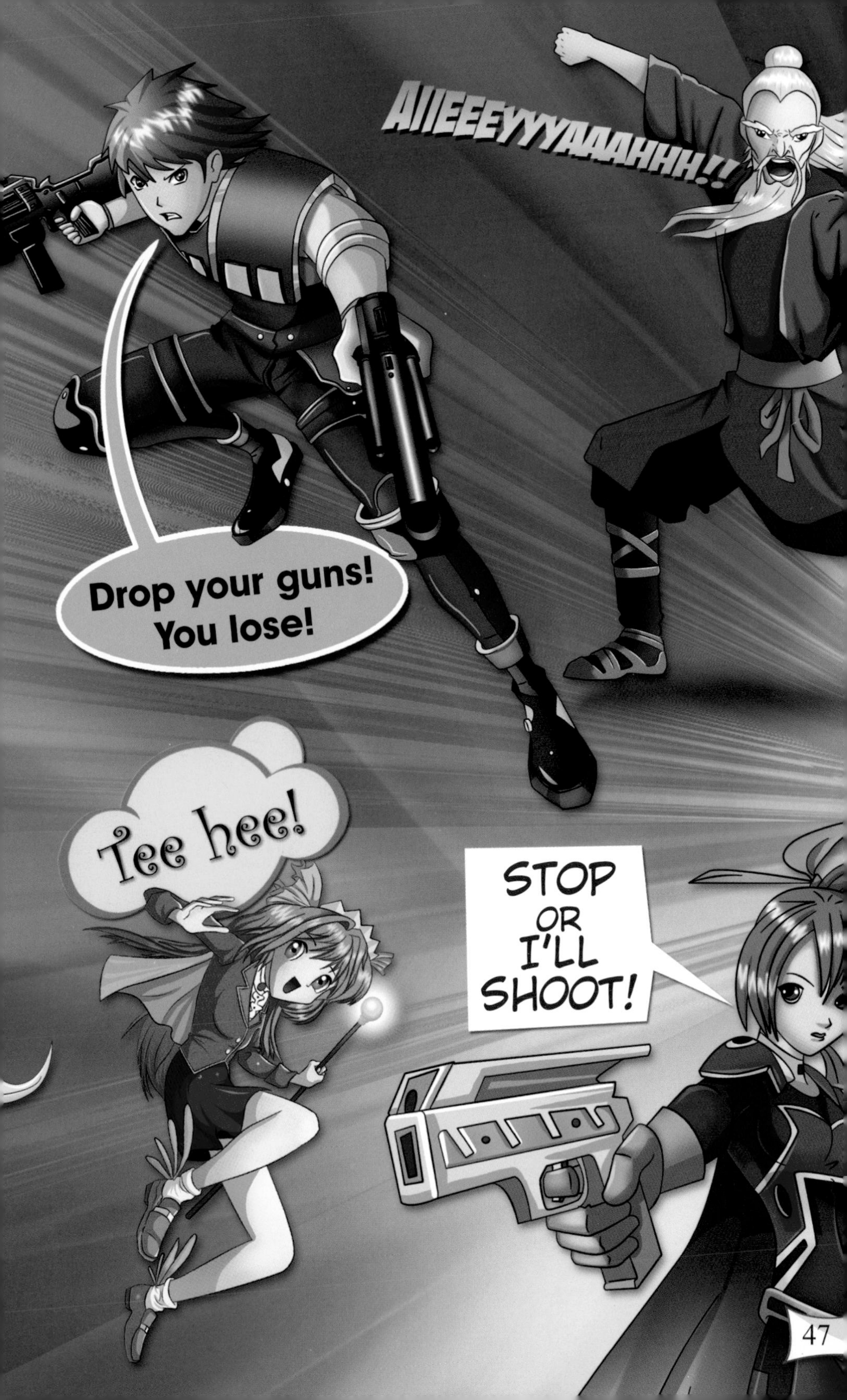
AIIEEEYYYAAAHHH!!
Drop your guns! You lose!
STOP OR I'LL SHOOT!
Tee hee!

# Read More

**Amberlyn, J. C.** *Drawing Manga: Animals, Chibis, and Other Adorable Creatures.* New York: Watson-Guptill, 2009.

**Besel, Jennifer M.** *The Captivating, Creative, Unusual History of Comic Books.* Unusual Histories. Mankato, Minn.: Capstone Press, 2010.

**Hart, Christopher.** *Kids Draw Big Book of Everything Manga.* New York: Watson-Guptill Publications, 2009.

**Orr, Tamra.** *Manga Artists.* Extreme Careers. New York: Rosen Pub., 2009.

**Sautter, Aaron.** *How to Draw Manga Warriors.* Drawing Cool Stuff. Mankato, Minn.: Capstone Press, 2008.

# Internet Sites

FactHound offers a safe, fun way to find Internet sites related to this book. All of the sites on FactHound have been researched by our staff.

Here's all you do:

Visit *www.facthound.com*

Type in this code: **9781429665933**